Praise for More of God

"In **More of God,** Betsy de Cruz writes with an engaging blend of personality, humor, spiritual depth, and practical help for equipping women to draw closer to God through a regular quiet time. Honest and relatable, Betsy shares her own challenges with distractions and unpacks a variety of strategies and tools for mental focus and increased depth in Bible reading, reflection, and prayer. With good instructions and creative ideas, Betsy fills our toolbox with both standard Bible study tips as well as many I have not seen before. I love discovering new ideas for enhancing my time with God!"
—**Ginger Harrington,** author of *Holy in the Moment: Simple Ways to Love God and Enjoy Your Life*, co-founder of Planting Roots: Strength to Thrive in Military Life

"I love Betsy's honesty about her own struggle with distraction in her daily walk with Christ—I can totally relate! Her book will help you create space and recapture the joy of regularly quieting your soul and basking in all that God has for you. My favorite quote? *'God whispers louder than the world's noise, if we'll only listen.'*"
—**Jenny Adams,** Women's Ministry Coordinator, Park Springs Bible Church, Arlington, Texas

"Betsy de Cruz helps distracted girls like me discover do-able strategies for Bible study. I loved the hands-on ideas to help me move from "dullsville" to "delight" by spending just 5 to 15 minutes a day in the Word. I will be taking a personal mini-retreat soon with my colored pencils and new prayer journal to create my prayer map. This book is a treasure, and I plan on sharing its practical wisdom with all my girlfriends."

—**Lyli Dunbar,** writer, speaker, and coach, Proverbs 31 Ministries First 5 writing team

"I have a short list of women I dream of meeting one day. Betsy is on that list. Her years of seeking God have rewarded her with a deep understanding of our King. This book shows how to discover "daily outpourings of fresh grace" by learning how to connect with God. The practical, down-to-earth tips Betsy shares are perfect for both new believers as well as more experienced Christ followers. I've come away with several new ideas I can't wait to implement! I highly recommend this book to any sister hungry for more of God."

—**Arabah Joy,** author of *Trust without Borders* and *Praying the Promises,* online mentor at Arabahjoy.com

"Though Betsy de Cruz and I have never met or lived in the same city, we are sisters in the same spiritual sorority. As a kid she wanted to be a nun; I wanted to be a monk. As adults we both hunger for quiet time and a closer relationship with God. But family-life, lengthy to-do lists, and short attention spans continue to vie for center stage. In her confessional, humorous, and wise book *More of God: A Distracted Woman's Guide to More Meaningful Quiet Times,* Betsy offers distracted soul sisters practical and accessible ways to return God to the center of our lives.

—**Sybil MacBeth,** author of *Praying in Color: Drawing A New Path to God* and *The Season of the Nativity: Confessions and Practices of an Advent, Christmas, and Epiphany Extremist.*

"Would you like to begin to really enjoy your life more? This book can help! Betsy de Cruz shows you how to find meaning in life by making more of your relationship with God. Through wonderful stories, Scripture, examples, and practical tips, you will discover how to create ample space in your life to enjoy God's presence. Whether you are a new believer or you've been walking with the Lord for years, you will benefit from reading these pages. I wholeheartedly recommend this book!"

—**Melanie Redd,** women's ministry leader and speaker, author of *How to Win Your Child's Heart for Life* and *Stepping Closer to the Savior*

"I was hooked from the first page of the introduction as if Betsy had a view into my own daily struggles to stay focused and keep prayer a priority each day. I write and teach about prayer, yet I, too, get distracted from prayer - regularly! I loved learning Betsy's approach to many of my personal favorite ways to pray, along with some new ideas I can't wait to try. If you struggle to focus in your prayers or pray consistently, you're not alone. Take heart from Betsy's down-to-earth encouragement and find more focus and depth in your prayers!"

—**Kathryn Shirey,** author of *Pray Deep: Ignite Your Prayer Life,* speaker, and prayer mentor at kathrynshirey.com

More of God

A Distracted Woman's Guide to More Meaningful Quiet Times

Betsy de Cruz

To Alev, Zeynep,
and all my believing sisters in Turkey.
It was my joy to learn from you how to pursue
God when the going gets tough.
I hold you in my heart.

Contents

Introduction:

A Letter from Me to You

I wrote this book because I imagine you might struggle with feeling distracted and overwhelmed as much as I do. So much about our daily lives can make us lose track of our relationship with God: busy schedules, responsibilities at work and home, and those constant cares and worries at the back of our minds. As if we didn't already have enough to think about, the internet brings distraction to a whole new level that women in generations past never had to deal with. Our phones buzz and beep constantly to let us know about texts from our kids, social media updates from our friends, and the latest breaking news events. Everyday life in the 21st century can drive a woman to distraction, and this affects our ability to draw near to God.

Yet He longs for us to recognize His voice and draw near, so He can fill us with His Spirit.

Whether it's caused by genetic tendencies or the fast pace of this crazy world we're living in, I suspect I have spiritual attention deficit. Even on good days, I can't pray for more than about two minutes without going off on a mental tangent, and when I try to read the Bible, sometimes my brain actually goes on a trip to Hawaii. If this is you too, I've written this with us in mind because I don't want either of us to let distraction stop us from going after more of God. To open our lives up to more of His presence, we can develop the art of focusing and drawing near to Him. I'm learning to pay attention to God one small step at a time, and I want to invite you to join me.

I've never been diagnosed with attention deficit, and perhaps you haven't either, but I bet you can relate when I tell you how absent-minded and scatterbrained I am. I'm the woman who leaves every kitchen cabinet and drawer open while cooking. My computer has 15 tabs open right now, and my phone constantly freezes up because I leave too many apps open. I'm usually working on 17 projects at the same time, finishing almost none of them. And yes, I'm that woman who looks straight at you when we meet yet can't remember your name ten seconds later. (*I'm sorry.*)

Scatterbrained. That's me. And let me tell you, it affects my spiritual life. I want more of God, but all too often I live distracted, and I bet the same thing happens to you.

I had a lightbulb moment about my spiritual life when my daughter was diagnosed with Attention Deficit Hyperactivity Disorder (ADHD) at age seventeen. The counsellor explained that girls with ADHD have hyperactive minds. Although they sit quietly in the classroom staring at the teacher, their minds flit from place to place and throw ideas around like a bouncing basketball on a court. The lightbulb came on for me when

I realized that's kind of what happens to me sometimes when I sit down to read my Bible or pray.

Even if we don't have attention deficit, our lives can make us feel like we're constantly battling distraction. Most women wear many hats and have too much to think about. We care for our families and homes while we also work in offices, classrooms, and laboratories. We wake up and walk around all day with a mental to-do list along the lines of this:

1. Locate five pairs of halfway clean socks
2. Buy laundry detergent
3. Get batteries for Tom's science project
4. Have the oil in the car changed
5. Pick up party invitations and plan Jim's birthday
6. Take dog to the vet
7. Help Kate with math homework
8. Reschedule dentist appointment
9. Call Mom

Our list goes on to include work-related tasks as well. All the while we're worried about a friend's battle with cancer, and we're checking our phones for news from her. Our natural tendency to distraction, worry, and frustration, coupled with our busy lives, make it easy to crowd God out.

GOOD NEWS FOR DISTRACTED WOMEN

The good news is we can learn to calm and quiet our souls. This book will focus on helping distracted women to enjoy a more meaningful connection with God and grow a stronger relationship with Him. For me, the best way to invite more of God into my life is through spending a short, focused time with Him each day.

Of course, our relationship with the Lord goes beyond our quiet time, but daily time with our Savior serves as a reset button for our souls, especially when we're struggling with weariness or worry. It's a training ground for us to learn to relate to God through worship, prayer, and reading His Word. Learning to focus on God and hear His voice in the morning sets us up to be more receptive to Him throughout our day.

> *Daily time with our Savior serves as a reset button for our souls.*

In this book I'll share with you how spending time with God each day makes a difference for me in my troubled times, and I hope you'll find encouragement to seek Him in your hard moments, too. More often than I can recount, it's during that daily quiet time when God gives me a word, a verse, or an encouragement that helps me get through a difficult day or season.

We can also laugh together at some of my ditzy, absent-minded moments. Like the other day when I went to the pharmacy with my daughter. Our pharmacy is a small, old-fashioned corner store where everything is behind the counter and you tell Karin what you need. When we walked in the door, I couldn't for the life of me remember what I'd gone in there for.

While Karin waited on the other customers, I stood in the middle of the shop with eyes narrowed, mentally going through all my lists. Suddenly it came to me, and I blurted out loudly:

"Contact Lens Solution!"

It came out sounding really weird, and I realized every eye in that shop was looking straight at me. Talk about socially awkward.

When we came out of the store, my daughter said, "Mom, didn't you even hear Karin say hello and ask how you are today? You just shouted out, "Lens solution!"

In that moment I felt like a total social misfit. Caught up in my own thoughts, I had been totally oblivious to our friend saying anything at all. How does someone walk into their neighborhood store and just shout out, "Contact lens solution!"?

Perhaps we do this with God as well. He longs to speak to us, but we're caught up in our own thoughts. He yearns to draw us to Himself and reveal His love for us, but we keep going a hundred miles a minute, stopping just to blurt out a desperate prayer once in a while.

I want more for my spiritual life than desperate prayer pit stops, so I've been challenged to think about how to quiet a mind racing with a thousand details in order to spend meaningful time with God each day. I've written this for myself and for you, if you're a woman who struggles with spiritual attention deficit. This is for you if you want to believe that God's promise holds true even for busy and distracted 21st century women:

"You will seek me and find me when you seek me with all your heart" (Jeremiah 29:13).

LET'S GO FOR MORE GRACE AND LESS GUILT

Can I be honest with you? I hesitated to write this book because the last thing you need is someone to guilt you into making time to read the Bible and pray. Too often, we look at quiet time with God as one more box to check off our "Good Christian Girl" to-do list. We view it as an obligation, something we *should* do and *would* do if we had it all together. Our thoughts go like this: "If good Christian women have a devotional time, and I'm having trouble fitting it into my schedule, maybe I'm not such a good Christian after all." Or, "If I'm bored when I read the Bible, and I keep checking for notifications on my phone, then I must be a 'Less Than' Christian." We feel guilty. We feel pressured to live up to some ideal, and when we don't measure up, we feel guilty again. We wonder if God really likes "Less Than" Christians.

If this is you, can I encourage you to relax and receive grace? God isn't looking for people who will read a page, recite a prayer, and check off a box. He's looking for basket-case people, like you and me, who'll admit to needing Him desperately. He's searching for people hungry for a deeper heart connection with Him. God is looking for people who are looking for Him. Of course, setting aside time to seek God through His Word and to learn to relate to Him through prayer is important, but there will be days when we can't actually sit down for that. We all have emergency room mornings, stressful weeks at work, or times when our kids are climbing into bed at 5:00 a.m. to ask for breakfast already. God sees that. He hears a quick, desperate prayer spoken out as you load your kids into the minivan, just as He hears the slow, quiet prayer at your kitchen table before anyone else is up at your house. So, on the chaos days let's receive "grace in place of grace already given" (John 1: 16).

WHAT YOU'LL FIND ON THESE PAGES

I invite you to join me as we take a look together at how we can get past distraction to find and experience more of God in our quiet times and in our lives as well. In the first chapter I'll share how time with God has been an anchor to my soul in the rough and rocky times of life, and then we'll continue in the following chapters to look at how giving God even 20 minutes a day can help us forge a stronger relationship with Him. I'll share some practical tips for finding focus, getting more goodness out of God's Word, and for making our quiet times more creative and enjoyable. We'll also look at ways to experience more of God by taking our quiet time blessings with us into the rest of the day, especially during hard times, and we'll consider ways women beset by distraction can actually pray. Friend, you and your relationship with God are the reason I wrote this book. I pray you'll find practical help and hope for your spiritual life on these pages.

INTRODUCTION

1

When You're not Rocking the Church Lady Thing

I might as well tell you right off the bat I'm no candidate for any Jesus Look-Alike prize. Many days I don't even look like a woman who spent time with Jesus in the morning. If someone gets on my nerves, I can snap and roll my eyes along with the best of them. Exasperation overtakes me when my beloved peeps leave their towels on the floor, and some nights worry overtakes me as I spend dark hours tossing, turning, and fretting instead of sleeping, which sets me up for more snapping and eye-rolling the next day. I'm telling you this right now as you start this book because I don't want you to think I'm pretending to rock this church lady thing.

Some days I feel like more like a "Dr. Jekyll and Mr. Hyde" woman than a Jesus Girl. Do you remember them? Dr. Jekyll is a scientist who mysteriously morphs into the ugly, evil Mr. Hyde after drinking a potion. The scary part is I don't even have to drink a magic potion to turn into my version of Mr. Hyde. On any given day, ordinary life experiences like broken vacuum cleaners, crying kids, unreasonable workmates, and long grocery lines can bring out the ugly in me.

Some weeks I am aware of a huge disconnect between how I act on Sunday morning at church and how I handle life on Tuesday out in a 100-degree parking lot when my car keys have mysteriously disappeared. Can you relate to feeling a disconnect between your Sunday morning self and your Monday-Friday self?

Who I am at Sunday worship service and who I am in line at the grocery store don't always look like the same woman. On Sunday morning I hear an encouraging message or experience God touching my heart and meeting my needs during worship, but my joy bubble bursts when my kids start complaining in the car after we drive out of the church parking lot. My faith falls flat on Friday when our refrigerator breaks down just after we finish paying the fifth medical bill of the month.

While I may not be rocking the church lady thing, I am learning to open the door of my heart to more of God. Because only God can grow my faith, give me the strength I need, and increase my joy. What's my secret to unlocking the door to a closer connection with God? Twenty minutes.

What helps me more than anything to tap into a life-transforming relationship with my Lord is to give Him at least twenty minutes of my day. More than going to church, listening to podcasts, or reading Christian books, spending twenty minutes a day with God helps me know Him better and more fully believe He loves me. More than a date with my husband or a friend, time with God restores my soul, helps me feel intimately known and cherished, and equips me with the strength I need to face the challenges life brings.

HOPE FOR HARD DAYS

 With each passing day, I realize more clearly how much I need to hang on to hope because otherwise trial and trouble can get me down. Have you noticed it too? Bad news can overwhelm. Sometimes life hands you a plate of hard knocks, but time with Jesus can infuse hope into your heart even on hard days.

Because I'm kind of slow, I didn't even discover how hard life was until I was 27 and my fiancé broke off our engagement. Up until then, everything I'd wanted had basically been handed to me. But on the thrilling day I bought my wedding dress and called to tell my fiancé about it, he told me he wasn't ready to marry me after all. In one moment, life did a roller coaster plunge from the heights of happiness to the depths of despair. After hanging up the phone, I cried for 24 hours straight; for a whole week I cried everywhere I went.

Instead of improving, life got worse when I developed Rheumatoid Arthritis months later. Debilitated and unable to walk or function, I spent six months at home, unable to work and still struggling to recover from a broken heart. By some strange mercy of God, the Bible was the only book I could read without physical pain. My Bible would lay open on my lap without my fingers having to hold its weight. On its pages I found hope.

"God, are you there, and do you really love me? Because if you really love me, why on earth is all this happening to me?" I asked. As I sat on the couch each morning with my Bible, I'd look at light coming in through the green and gold leaves outside my window, and I'd ask God my hard questions. Just as light illuminated those leaves, God's Spirit brought His Word to life and spoke hope into my heart through words such as these:

"I have loved you with an everlasting love; I have drawn you with unfailing kindness. I will build you up again." (Jeremiah 31:3,4a)

"For I know the plans I have for you... plans to prosper you and not to harm you, plans to give you hope and a future." (Jeremiah 29:11)

When everything I thought I knew about life and God went topsy-turvy on me, God's Word gave me a firm place to stand. My feelings were all over the planet, but God's truth remained the same. I repeated to myself along with the Psalmist: "But I trust in your unfailing love; my heart rejoices in your salvation. I will sing the Lord's praise, for he has been good to me" (Psalm 13:5, 6). I didn't feel it. My unhinged emotions were knocking me upside down, but as I read it and said it, I began to believe it. Hope grew inside me. I could trust Him because somehow I knew He loved me.

HELP WHEN WE NEED IT

Not only do I need hope, I also need all the help I can get. After José and I finally married four years after breaking off our engagement, we discovered the challenges of raising two kids. Children add so much joy to our lives, but they also drive us stark raving mad by keeping us up all night when they're babies and bringing the mess in our homes to a whole new level when they're toddlers. Then they ask us to teach them to drive when they're teenagers. During those challenges, I learned that God will get us through if we stick close to Him.

The peace Jesus gives doesn't depend on a quiet, orderly house or a relaxed schedule. It's available 24/7 when we call on Him or sit down for even two minutes to ask Him to fill our hearts.

When my son was born, I soon realized motherhood was my greatest joy and nightmare. During those first weeks of learning to care for the small being that ruled my world and made me feel like a sleep-deprived, crazy woman who didn't know what she was doing, I needed God desperately. While walking the hall one night at 2 a.m. with my screaming infant, a horrifying idea came to me: "I wonder if he'd be quiet if I threw him against the wall." I felt like the worst mother in the world.

After several weeks of struggling and feeling guilty for entertaining such terrible thoughts, I finally talked to my husband about my violent, angry feelings. Admitting to those thoughts and emotions was hard, but surprisingly, my husband confessed he'd had them as well. When we sat down together to ask God to cleanse our thoughts, protect us from Satan's influence, and strengthen our hearts, He responded. I don't know what God did as my husband and I prayed together, but miraculously I never had such thoughts of violence towards my kids again.

In the days to follow, I learned that no matter how much frustration erupted in my heart, I could always come back to God to center my thoughts on His Word. Even a few minutes could change the course of a bad day and somehow equip me with the patience I needed to make it until that child's next nap.

Even now, with an empty nest and both kids at college, I desperately need a fresh outpouring of God's love, joy, and peace every single day. God has everything I need, but it's up to me to seek Him every day, not simply on Sunday mornings. I'm discovering that having young adult children means you have more problems to worry about: yours and theirs! It's a whole new level of challenges.

I need daily grace to let go of control and trust God. Even when I can't see Him working as I'd like, I need faith to trust Him. Small daily doses of God's presence and power restore my faith and help me receive His love, joy, and peace.

> *Small daily doses of God's presence and power build our faith.*

GRACE FOR OUR GRITTY LIVES

Even a few minutes reading God's Word each day strengthens us to do hard things. His Word fed my faith and literally kept me alive and relatively joyful during 17 years of serving in the Middle East. My husband and I recently returned to America, but while we lived alongside 75,000,000 dear Muslim people, almost nothing in the environment encouraged my faith. Depression was rampant, and domestic violence was an everyday occurrence. Indeed, sometimes we heard it behind closed doors in our apartment building. When I shared my faith, few people expressed interest, but Scripture reminded me that my job was to plant the seed and trust God to water it in His timing.

Even back in the days before Kindle and online podcasts and blogs, God spoke to me each morning through the Bible to keep my faith and hope alive. A close connection with Him sustained me each day in a land where most Christian workers return home after only two or three years due to discouragement. We tasted bitter disappointment when my husband still struggled to speak the language after five years, when friends rejected us after we shared the gospel, and when disciples we poured our lives into left the Christian faith. We learned to find our joy in God and in the small fruit of a few changed and beautiful lives.

My husband and I are no better than any of our co-workers who returned home sooner than we did; undoubtedly God had a different call for them. All I know is we couldn't have survived 17 years in a spiritual desert without daily outpourings of fresh grace. I spent over half my Christian life in a Muslim land, and I couldn't have continued growing as a believer without God's Spirit watering my faith and His Word teaching me how to "be strong in the grace that is in Christ Jesus" (2 Timothy 2:1). Even on those days when juggling my children, home, and ministry meant I only had a few minutes to intentionally seek Him.

LESS GUILT AND MORE JOY

Your life has its own brand of grit, and you might not be able to relate to my challenges at all. You have your own worries that keep you up at 2:00 am. and your own people who drive you crazy or hurt your heart. You have your personal routines and schedules that stress you beyond belief on a bad day. You've probably also discovered you don't always get what you want in this life, and you're on a unique, personal journey to pursue love and happiness as best you can.

Friend, our lives look different, but if you've put your faith in Jesus Christ, we have the same Savior. We have the same God who waits for us to come home when our hearts stray from Him. We have the same Holy Spirit who seals our redemption and guarantees our inheritance in the same heavenly home.

God longs for us to know Him better, not just as an intellectual pursuit, but so we can actually experience more of Him in our lives. Our Heavenly Father yearns to scoop us up when we're hurting and pour grace into our aching, empty places. He wants to strengthen us for the challenges in front of us. Jesus stands ready to come when we call out to Him.

Our Heavenly Father yearns to pour grace into our aching places.

A DOORWAY TO CLOSER CONNECTION

When I first became a Christian at age 18, an older friend gave me a little booklet with questions for every chapter in the book of John. The mornings when I could manage it, I sat down and penciled in answers in the blank spaces of that booklet. I'm grateful for that person who encouraged me and started me off on a life-long process of getting to know God better. But thinking about that now, I realize I need more than a "check-off-the-box" faith, and I want a relationship with God that goes beyond "fill-in-the-blank" conversations. I want more for you too.

I yearn for a deeper heart connection with God, my constant Companion who promises to never leave me. I need His love to fill my heart on the lonely days. I want to hear the Voice that whispers, "And hope does not put us to shame, because God's love has been poured out into our hearts through the Holy Spirit, who has been given to us." (Romans 5:5). Sometimes I need to just sit with His love and receive it, believe it. I want joy that brings a smile to my face. I long for peace that calms my fears and helps me know deep inside everything is going to be okay.

I want more. More of God.

I want it for you too, friend. So I invite you on a journey to draw closer and go deeper. A journey to open the door to more of God. This journey starts with taking a look around to see where we are and what's keeping us from experiencing a closer connection with Him

2

Living Distracted and Moving Past It

I let distraction keep me from doing many things I want to do. For example, I meant for a long time to sit down and write a book to help women find a more focused, meaningful connection with God, but each day distraction got in my way. Just when I started to think about my book idea, the phone would ring, but I couldn't actually answer it because one of my kids needed help right then. Later I'd realize it was my turn to cook for Thursday night Bible study, and I had a writing assignment due, and a loud buzzer signaled that I'd better get my clothes out of the dryer before they wrinkled. When I'd finally get through those, I'd notice Facebook telling me I had 35 notifications, so for months, I never got around to starting this book.

So it is with time to read God's Word or talk with Him. Whether we actually struggle with attention deficit or not, everyday life in our crazy world can literally drive us to distraction. Although we desperately need more of God in our lives, the shiny, loud, urgent, and desperate things of this world take our attention away from Him. Daily life calls, and quiet time slips through my fingers as I run around like a chicken with its head cut off tackling items on my to-do list against the backdrop of constant interruptions. Yet the only way to grow closer to God is to pay attention, to quiet the world and turn our focus to Him.

Jesus continues to call us: "Behold, I stand at the door and knock. If anyone hears my voice and opens the door, I will come in to him and eat with him, and he with me" (Revelation 3:20, ESV). While we live distracted, our Savior lives with focus. His attention fully on us, Jesus stands waiting until we invite Him in. What a promise! If we hear His voice and open the door, He'll come in. Yet that voice is not always easy to perceive. Let's look at some of the things that keep us from hearing it.

While we live distracted, our Savior's attention is fixed on us.

SOCIAL MEDIA: THE WORLD IN OUR FACES

My phone distracts me from hearing God's voice more than anything else does. Through social media, the world bangs loudly at the door of our hearts and pulls us in. For years, I was blissfully ignorant, and I resisted getting a cell phone. Why would I want to carry around a little machine that beeped and buzzed and exerted control over me? When it became absolutely necessary, I purchased the simplest flip phone I could find. While other people tapped and swiped their smart phones, I was content and happy with my dumbphone. I even judged friends who texted and checked notifications while they were with me. When I finally broke down and bought a phone, I wondered how I'd ever lived without it, but I had no idea it would bring distraction to a whole new level in my life.

I didn't know a woman could get pulled into an endless trap of checking notifications and scrolling through feeds until her brain got overloaded enough to short circuit. I didn't know you could hop onto Pinterest to look for a recipe and find yourself still there an hour later. And I certainly didn't know those little notification numbers on my home screen would entice me to log on multiple times in one hour just to see what my friend Kristi had commented about my post and what my son or daughter had just posted.

I didn't know how a constant barrage of news headlines can drain the hope and light right out of a woman, making her feel like the world is a dismal place and where is God anyway? Do you ever take advantage of a free moment thinking you'll relax by looking at social media only to end up feeling more tired and stressed?

God whispers louder than the world's noise, if we'll only listen. He says, "Be still. Be still and know that I am God" (Psalm 46:10a). For a woman wired like I am, being still is hard. I can hardly sit still to watch a television program, let alone get my soul still before God. But I'm learning. Before I look at social media in the morning, I'm learning to set my mind on His Word, so I can start the day with a stilled heart.

> *God whispers louder than the world's noise, if we'll only listen.*

Also, I'm learning that later in the day, I can help my soul be still by choosing to listen to a worship song or sit for a few quiet moments instead of filling every spare minute with a scroll through my social media feed. When I take a moment to intentionally focus on God, it helps me keep my heart in tune with Him as I continue my activities.

TOO BUSY FOR GOD

Sometimes we're just too busy to pay much attention to our Savior. Ask someone how they're doing, and more likely than not they'll answer back, "Tired" or "Busy." For some reason, we've been tricked into thinking busy is better because it makes us valuable. We work all week, volunteer when called on, and cart our kids around to evening and weekend activities. More activities, projects, and social events help us feel more significant. Busy has become our new normal, but it can distract us from investing time in what's really important: spiritual renewal, relationships, and our best work.

We've even been tricked into thinking our Christian activities define our relationship with God. So we teach Sunday school, join the women's Bible study, sing in the Easter choir, and volunteer to serve in the after school program. Of course, our service honors God and builds His church, but I confess more than once I've committed myself to do something "for God" without even asking Him if He wanted me to do it in the first place. Instead of resting in my identity as child of God, I act like a slave who needs to work to please Him. I forget my Heavenly Father wants children first. Surely He values the time we spend *with* Him just as much as or more than the things we do *for* Him. Busyness can distract us from our relationship with God.

When I began writing this book, I was coming through a busy season. My family had moved through eight time zones to relocate back to our Middle East home after nine months stateside. The weeks preceding our move were filled with several trips, packing, and goodbyes. After we arrived home to Turkey, my days flew by unpacking boxes and suitcases. I had to relearn daily life all over again, with housework, shopping, and cooking in a country where convenience was not a thing.

Two years later we made that move again in reverse, and now I'm having to relearn life in America, but my daily schedule still hasn't settled down. Juggling family, ministry, and writing keep me more than busy; they'll keep me frantic if I let them.

Writing this book actually taught me something. Just as I wrote it by sitting my rear end down in a chair, turning off my phone, and focusing for 25-minute time slots, so can I forge a better connection with God by focusing on Him for two minutes, three minutes, or five, whatever I'm able to give. Sometimes forcing myself to stop for three minutes to read one Bible verse and pray can turn negative thoughts or a bad day around.

Jesus never gives up on me; He gives me an open invitation. "Come to me, all you who are weary and burdened, and I will give you rest. Take my yoke upon you and learn from me, for I am gentle and humble in heart, and you will find rest for your souls." (Matthew 11:28,29) Honestly, I don't always listen. Some days I hear His voice, but I rush on by. Yet I'm learning that when I stop to listen and draw near, He comes with just what I need.

When I stop to draw near to Jesus,
He comes with just what I need.

DERAILED BY DISAPPOINTMENT

A friend of mine recently confessed she needed help for her soul-crushing times. I could understand where she was coming from, and I bet you can too. We've all been in that place of wondering, "God, why aren't you coming through for me? Did you hear my prayer? If you did, why didn't you do anything about it?" Even when it feels like God has let us down, it seems wrong to say it because He's God, right? So we keep silent about our disappointments. We quietly lower our expectations and drift away from Him. Why bother seeking him if He doesn't really come through for us?

A few years ago, my husband and I invested valuable time in a younger couple that came to the Lord out of a Muslim background. After their baptism, we met with them every Thursday night for Bible study and prayer for a whole year. We loved this couple dearly and enjoyed our times together. Yet about six months after their conversion, we began to notice they found it easier to complain about and criticize others rather than admit to their own shortcomings. They hit a wall in their Christian growth because they couldn't recognize their own sin.

We prayed earnestly, but instead of seeing results, we watched this couple drift further away. They stopped coming on Thursday nights and later left the church altogether. Our hopes faded, and we wondered if we'd wasted all the time and love we'd invested in them. Where were the answers to our prayers?

I'm sure you have your share of disappointments too. We all experience failed work projects, ministry efforts that go sour, sick children who don't get better, financial pressure, and job loss. Disappointment can derail us. It's hard to believe God loves us when He lets us go through hard times. We assume maybe He doesn't care about us as much as we thought, and we're tempted to give up seeking Him because it didn't really get us anywhere in the first place. It's easy to drift away from our first love.

When disappointment threatens to undo my faith, what enables me to keep turning back to God is to get real with Him. I can bring those disappointments to Him and pour out my anger, doubt, and worry, trusting my Father cares for me. Maybe we hold our negative emotions back from God because we're somehow scared lightning will strike us down, but He can take it. If we hold on to shallow faith that refuses to acknowledge struggles and doubts, we end up feeling further from God. Getting real with God in times of hurt ultimately helps us to develop a closer relationship with Him.

Two years ago, my family went through crushing times as one of our teen children suffered devastation. The Lord brought this verse to mind again and again: "The LORD is close to the brokenhearted and saves those who are crushed in spirit" (Psalm 34:18). I'll talk more about persevering with God through disappointments later in the book, but for now I want to share one thing I've discovered: When I bring my broken heart to God, He shows Himself close to me. He leans in and whispers words of hope. Sometimes it takes a few days or weeks, but closeness between us grows again when I stick to reading even a simple Psalm each day. I begin to feel His love for me in new ways.

When I bring my broken heart to God, He leans in and whispers words of hope.

DISTRACTED BY THE DOLDRUMS

Some days God feels a million miles away, and picking up a Bible seems like the last thing on earth you'd want to do. After all, Pinterest is much more colorful and entertaining than snoozing through your "Bible in One Year" reading plan. Here's where the sheer discipline of showing up can get you through. In my own life, I've experienced both times of persevering to stick with God when prayer seems boring and times of breakthrough. What I know is that usually the breakthrough comes after the persevering.

Maybe we miss out on more of God because we settle in and expect less. After all, the Bible is not always easy and entertaining, so we read it a bit less. We wonder if God really answers our prayers, so we pray less. We go to church on Sundays but it's easy to leave our faith there when we walk out the door. We can pick it up again when we come back next week. Before we know it, we get a bad case of spiritual doldrums.

Rather than settling for less, I want to press in for more. And when God seems distant, maybe that's when we need to get real with Him and say, "Forgive me, but right now reading the Bible makes me yawn. Could you bring this to life for me? Could you speak to me while I read it? I want to hear from you." Surely God loves daring prayers like this: "I've been praying, but I don't see any answers. Would you please give me a specific answer, so I can know you're really there? Would you let me know today that you hear me?" In many of my desperate times, when my faith lags low, I pray that prayer. Amazingly, God has mercy and responds when I start praying specifically.

The story of Gideon encourages me because Gideon gets real with God. At the beginning of the story in Judges 6, Gideon has every right to be in a funk. The Midianites have oppressed Israel for seven years, reducing the Israelites to poverty. Terrorizing the land, they steal crops and livestock. In fact, Gideon is hiding out in a winepress when the angel of the Lord appears to him and says, "The Lord is with you, mighty warrior" (Judges 6:12). Gideon's response almost makes me laugh because it sounds like something that could come out of my own mouth.

"Pardon me, my lord," Gideon replies, "but if the Lord is with us, why has all this happened to us?" (Judges 6:13) Gideon gets real with God. He asks a question a lot of us think but sometimes can't bring ourselves to ask the Lord. "Why has all this happened?" Then we read next how the Lord calls Gideon to save Israel and Gideon questions Him again, "Pardon me, my lord, but how can I save Israel?" (Judges 6:15) This dialogue represents the way I want to talk with God when I'm not sure He's really there. "Pardon me, Lord. Forgive my unbelief, but could You show yourself to me today? I need Your grace and mercy in order to keep believing." Bold and honest prayer can get us out of the doldrums.

Later, Gideon gets even more audacious with God. Shortly before battle, he asks God for reassurance in the boldest of ways. Gideon places a wool fleece on the ground and asks God to make the fleece wet with dew and the ground around it dry. If God does that, it will be a sign to Gideon that God is sending him. God grants the little miracle Gideon asks for, but even then Gideon needs still more reassurance; he says, "Do not be angry with me. Let me make just one more request." This time he asks that the ground be covered with dew and the fleece kept dry. Amazingly, God again does just what he asks (Gideon 6:36-40). Then Gideon, fully assured, goes into battle and wins the victory God calls him to

Maybe we also need to get real and get bold with God. Years ago, I started letting God know when I felt doubt. When I wasn't recognizing any answers to big, broad prayers, I started to pray specifically, and let God know I needed a small sign.

Last year, I felt discouraged when a young woman I'd sensed God call me to invest in dropped out of the Christian faith altogether. I wondered if I'd made the whole thing up, so I prayed. "Lord, did you even call me to do this? If you hear me and want me to continue praying for and reaching out to this girl, please give me a sign. I need to hear from you." Two hours later, she called me, the first time she'd done so in six months. It was small, but to me it was a sign nonetheless.

Another time recently, I was feeling blah, so I prayed for God to encourage me in some way that day. I didn't have anything specific in mind. Three hours later a friend sent me a gift bag full of cosmetics and perfume for no reason at all, and I remembered my prayer.

Gideon shows us a powerful model of someone who responds honestly to God and prays simple, specific prayers.

While I truly believe God loves to answer those "I'm down to the wire; are You there?" prayers, there are other times when He chooses to remain silent. Sometimes we just have to persevere in holding on to God's promise to open His door to those who knock and reward those who seek Him. However, let's not forget the life principle Gideon offers to us: When we get real with God, He becomes more real to us.

When we get real with God, He becomes more real to us.

So many things get in the way of our experiencing a meaningful relationship with God, a relationship that spills over into our everyday and transforms our lives. Distraction, busyness, disappointment, and plain old boredom can lead us to feel distant from Him.

The best way I know to overcome these obstacles, or persevere through them, is to seek a heart connection with God. When we open our hearts to Him, He comes in. This may sound unattainable, like high and mighty pie in the sky, but all it takes is a five-minute effort when we're at the end of our rope. All it takes is to cry out the name of Jesus when we're desperate. Little by little, our connection with God grows and spills into our lives.

3

How 20 Minutes a Day Can Change Your Life

Back in fifth grade, I shocked the Methodist Sunday school teacher when I announced to the class that I wanted to be a nun when I grew up. I didn't get why he was so surprised. How could I know Methodist girls didn't grow up to be Catholic nuns? I didn't know what nuns did, but I'd seen a television show where it looked like they loved God and lived peaceful lives serving Him, helping people, and praying with tranquil expressions on their faces. For some reason, it looked like a good life to me.

Looking back, I realize now that even when I was a child, God put in my heart a small glimmer of desire to know Him. Growing up, my family basically went to church on Christmas and Easter, yet that example of living faith I saw in those nuns on TV drew my attention.

So far God hasn't called me to be a nun, but He has called me to be His friend and given me a desire to draw near to Him. My all-time favorite book—based on the work of a 17th century monk, see the connection?—is

41

Practicing the Presence of God: Brother Lawrence for Today's Reader. That phrase, "practicing the presence of God," has stuck with me for most of my Christian life. Brother Lawrence worked in a kitchen, and I love his vision for continual communion with Jesus and practicing "His presence in my everyday amidst the clanging and banging of pots."[1] I also want to connect with God in my everyday life while I work, cook, eat, type, and make phone calls.

Sometimes I envy those nuns because I reason that seeking a close relationship with God must be easier for them since they have more time at their disposal to sit at His feet and learn how to pray. However, the more I think about it, the more I realize they also must get distracted. Because anyone can get bored sitting all by themselves for an hour, right?

LEARNING TO CONNECT WITH GOD

My life is different from a contemplative nun's life, and I know yours probably is too. But we all have the same basic need to learn to draw closer to God and see Him transform our lives. He is always near, waiting for us. We're the ones who stray from His path, run ahead of Him, totally forget about Him, and get lost on our way. But we can always return to our Father who waits for us with open arms. We can learn to listen and talk to Him. We can learn to pay attention to God a few minutes at a time.

Setting aside 20 minutes each morning gives me the chance to grow the skill of paying attention. I like to call it quiet time because it opens up space in my life to rest from the noise of the world and get quiet with Jesus. In 15 or 20 minutes, I often find a heart connection with my Lord that leads to a more intimate, focused relationship with Him for the rest of the day.

It's a micro-learning time for me to experiment and learn to relate to my Savior. For me, 20 minutes often turn into 30, but for you, 20 minutes might be too long. Perhaps you might experiment with five minutes. How long we do it doesn't matter nearly as much as developing a daily habit of drawing near to pay attention.

For me, daily time with God each morning opens the door to more peace and joy. So encouraging other women to invest time in their relationship with God and to learn to hear His voice through His Word is my biggest passion. It's the reason I wrote this book: to encourage people like you to experience more meaningful quiet time with God and carry that experience into the rest of your day.

REMEMBERING WHY

As I mentioned before, the last thing I want to do is lay one more burden on busy women; we don't need one more obligation to fulfill to be "good" Christian women. You may be struggling under what feels like a soul-numbing burden of responsibility as you try to balance your day job and family. After working hard each day at the office, you come home to corral your kids, make meals for them, help them with homework, and referee their fights.

Perhaps you spend your weekends driving them to all those activities our culture tells you they need in order to grow up to be fulfilled, happy adults. Then you remember you're supposed to spend quality time with them too.

Maybe you serve in full-time ministry, and the needs of others overwhelm. Quiet time with God can sink down to the bottom of our priority list because it's not so urgent as the other demands that press upon us daily.

As busy women, we keep ourselves organized by making lists of what we need to do, and seeing the results gives us a feeling of fulfillment. Yet we rarely get a sense of accomplishment after we sit down to be quiet with God for a few minutes because we might not see instant results. Mop the floor, and at least it stays clean until dinner time. Spend a few minutes reading the Bible or trying to pray, and the frustrating thing is you don't always see tangible results. After ten minutes reading Scripture, you might feel more peace for about 45 seconds if you're like me.

We forget that the fruit of investing in our relationship with God only becomes visible over time. When we spend time with Him, His Spirit works slow change in us.

Spending time with God each day creates a space in our lives for more of Him. Our relationship with Him grows. We open ourselves up in a focused way to let God refuel us and renew our faith. When we remember our why, our time with God becomes more meaningful.

> Spending time with God creates a space in our lives for more of Him.

God wants a relationship with us.

Years ago, a younger Christian woman and I gave a workshop on quiet time at a women's retreat. When we met beforehand to plan our seminar, she wanted to call it "Date with God." At first I thought that sounded more than weird, but her enthusiasm convinced me. As a single woman, she wanted to view her quiet time with God as a special time to look forward to, just as she would get excited about a date with a man she was interested in.

My friend later married, and now we have an easy accountability to encourage each other to keep dating our husbands. I've seen that regular dates with my husband are a healthy anchor to our relationship. They provide a time to have fun together as well as an opportunity for deep conversation. The two hours I spend with my husband on Wednesday night carry over into the rest of my week. When we let date time slide, we also then tend to start forgetting to make communication and closeness top priorities in our marriage.

The God of the universe created us for a privileged relationship with Him, but it's easy to take this for granted. God loves relating to us. When He created Adam and Eve, He walked with them in the garden. God called Abraham His friend, and He spoke with Moses face to face. He wants that kind of walking, talking, and living relationship with us too, but sometimes we're too busy to make time for Him. Just like warm fuzzies from my date with my husband carry over into the rest of my week, so do the benefits of morning time with God spill over into the rest of my day and life.

*Benefits of morning time with God
spill over into the rest of my day.*

"I have called you friends," Jesus said. "For everything that I learned from my Father I have made known to you" (John 15:15). I'm amazed that Jesus calls us His friends. He gives us an open invitation to relationship. Let's look again at His words in Revelation 3:20: "Behold, I stand at the door and knock. If anyone hears my voice and opens the door, I will come in to him and eat with him, and he with me." When I read these words, I want to accept His invitation and honor our relationship by setting aside time for Him. For me, that time presents an opportunity to learn how to relate to my Lord. When I spend time trying to listen or talk to Jesus in my quiet time, I'm more likely to check in with Him later in the day as well.

Time with God refuels us for the day ahead

Back in my high school days, I used to run out of gas all the time. My poor father, a true saint, kept the gas can handy because he never knew when he'd have to use it. I'd run out of gas on the way to school, or on the way home from a party late at night. It made for a good story at my wedding reception, and now we all laugh about it. Looking back thirty years later, I'm amazed that Dad always showed up with that gas can.

Just like a car can't go very far unless the driver stops for frequent refueling, believers can't get very far on their faith journey without filling their spiritual tanks. With all the troubling news we read every day in today's world, our own faith won't get us very far unless we fuel it with God's Word. Under the weight of responsibilities, our strength lags. On our own efforts, we can't conjure up the hope, wisdom, and encouragement we need. We run out of them, and just like my Dad showed up for me, our Heavenly Father shows up to give us what we need when we seek Him. We need to go to God daily for refueling.

The same God who spoke to the Israelites in the desert speaks to us today, "For it was I, the Lord your God, who rescued you from the land of Egypt. Open your mouth wide, and I will fill it with good things" (Psalm 81:10, NLT). Just as God promised to care for His people and give them all they needed long ago, so He is faithful to fill us up with good things today. When we seek Him, He refreshes us. When we spend time in His Word, He renews our hope and faith; He fills our hearts with His love, so we can give to others. When we ask for renewed strength, He pours out His power. He fills us with joy and peace as we choose to trust Him.

When we ask God for renewed strength, He pours out His power.

Renewed Faith When Life Gets Tough

Just like you, I've gone through many times when my faith takes a hit, but the summer of 2016 took the cake. My faith hit rock bottom. Our year stateside had been one of our hardest ever: a lemon car drained our bank account, and a two-month cancer scare rocked our faith and drained our bank account further. When we returned to our Middle Eastern home, a military coup attempt rocked the nation. A blanket of fear and uncertainty settled over the whole country.

Then our refrigerator broke, leaving us five days with no way to keep groceries cold. We cried out to God for encouragement and provision as never before, and the last straw came when we learned our salary for July would be 30% less than usual. For the first time in our married lives, we didn't know how we'd feed our kids until the end of the month. But we held on.

Each morning I wrestled with God. I fought to keep bitterness at bay, and I prayed for a grateful spirit. And each morning, I'd receive the encouragement I needed to make it through the day in one piece. I'd find a verse from my daily Bible reading that fed my faith. Or I'd listen to a worship song that touched my spirit.

I'd reach for God each morning, and He'd continue to reach me later in the day. He used my own daughter to encourage me during lunch one day. She suggested we sing the song "Blessed Be Your Name"[2] at the table, so we joined her, with hands raised around that table in a hot kitchen with no refrigerator. And as we sang, God strengthened our hearts.

But one morning I read something that jumped off the page of my Bible and changed my outlook for weeks to come:

"Against all hope, Abraham in hope believed and so became the father of many nations, just as it had been said to him, 'So shall your offspring be.'

48

Without weakening in his faith, he faced the fact that his body was as good as dead—since he was about a hundred years old—and that Sarah's womb was also dead. Yet he did not waver through unbelief regarding the promise of God, but was strengthened in his faith and gave glory to God, being fully persuaded that God had power to do what he had promised." (Romans 4:18-21)

As I read these words describing the faith crisis of Abraham, my own faith was strengthened. When I thought about the obstacles Abraham faced to become the father of nations, the first being infertility and old age, I realized perhaps my own challenges paled in comparison.

If Abraham did not waver through unbelief, I could pray for God to strengthen my faith too. Romans 10:17 says, "Faith comes by hearing, and hearing by the word of God," and when my faith hit rock bottom, God's Word renewed it in a way I simply cannot explain. Call it supernatural. It happened in one of those 20-minute time slots with God and carried over into the rest of the month. (By the way, God provided everything we needed during that crisis time. We later discovered our company had made an accounting error in our salary, and I wondered if God didn't allow it to bring me to my Romans 4 faith moment.)

Remembering our why —better relationship, refueling, and renewed faith— can keep our quiet times fresher and more meaningful as we pray for God to work His way in us. Friend, let's pray that God will draw us to Himself and deepen our relationship with Him. Let's ask Him to fill us up with what we need to live effective and joyful Christian lives.

20 MINUTES IS A SPRINGBOARD TO MORE

Some friends tell me setting aside a specific time for God each morning is just not the way they're wired. They don't want to limit their relationship with Jesus to a specific time frame and prefer instead to talk to Him throughout the day. Of course, everyone's spiritual walk is different, and each person needs to discover their own path to finding more of God while staying true to the way He created them. And yes, surely friendship with God goes far beyond setting aside 20 minutes for Him in the morning.

Ideally, we should walk and talk with God all day, but for me that's hard to do cold turkey. Instead, spending time with Him each morning makes it more likely that I'll return to Him or call on Him later in the day. And during those frantic times in life when I just can't seem to stop a moment to pray or remember He's with me, at least I had time with Him in the morning.

In her book *Enjoying the Presence of God*, Jan Johnson writes, "A quiet time trains us to focus and to hear God — skills necessary to enjoy God's presence."[3] When we learn to discern His voice during those 20 minutes, we recognize it more easily during the rest of the day. When we practice praising Him in our quiet time, worship comes to us more easily at other times as well. When we learn to give God our worries first thing in the morning, prayer for our concerns comes more naturally later in the day.

When we give God our worries in the morning, prayer for our concerns comes more naturally later in the day.

During our quiet time we learn or practice how to relate to God. I like to look at it as a springboard to experiencing more of Him later in my day. Twenty minutes we spend with Him in the morning can impact our whole day. For the rest of this book, we'll look at how to make that time more meaningful and how to keep walking with God throughout the day.

4

Making Space for God

One thing I loved about living in the Middle East was the hospitality. If I knocked on a neighbor's door, nine times out of ten, they'd invite me in for a cup of coffee. When I ran into someone I knew on the street, they'd say, "Come for a visit. We're waiting for you." And when I walked up the stairs to our third story apartment, I'd see all the shoes on my neighbors' doormats, a sure sign that friends or family had come to visit. I want to have that same welcoming spirit that throws open the doors of heart and home to other people. Perhaps it's because I love the warm feeling I get when someone welcomes me into their home. Don't you?

I want to be one of the welcomers. They're the ones always ready to pull up an extra chair for someone else to join in at the table. I want to be willing to open room in my heart for people who might need a safe place there; in the same way, I long to make room for God. On a daily basis, I want to create space for Him in my life, to invite Him in and let Him know He has a special place in my heart.

> *I want to create space for God in my life and let Him know He has a special place in my heart.*

But somehow life goes by at breakneck speed, pulling me with it. Responsibilities, worries, and the needs of people around me crowd God out unless I get intentional about making room in my life and inviting Him in.

MAKING TIME FOR GOD

My friend Amy thrives on busyness. She somehow manages to combine full-time secular work with almost full-time Christian ministry. She and her husband have plans every night of the week, and she's gloriously happy that way (when she's not exhausted). Yet I'm always amazed how she manages to carve out time for her friends. Our lives have taken different roads into separate friendship and ministry circles, but we still manage to find the time to sit down together once in a while. A two-hour coffee date with her is a friendship offering that brings joy to my heart, partly because I know it involves valuable effort on her part to make time for me.

When we put the brakes on our busy lives for a few minutes to make time for God, I imagine it brings joy to His heart as well. To slow down, learn to pay attention, and establish a heart connection with our Lord, we have to give Him some of our time. How much we're able to give depends on our situation. It's not so much how many minutes we spend as it is the quality and consistency of the time we invest.

Remember the poor widow who put two copper coins into the offering? Next to the large amounts thrown into the treasury by the wealthy, her offering might have looked like nothing. Yet Jesus valued it. He marveled that she had put in all she had to live on (Mark 12:41-44).

Perhaps in the same way He takes special delight when a mom with a newborn and two littles manages to sit down for five minutes with Him. Surely He rejoices as well in the five minutes given by a single mom of three high schoolers who cares for her aging parents. Jesus looks at our hearts, not at our pocket books and schedules.

I imagine most busy women are like me: constantly thinking about how long things might take and how to schedule everything in. And if you're also distracted like me, you might find it hard to focus on one thing at a time because you're always thinking about what's next.

If that is you, you might try this tip to help yourself learn to center your thoughts on God: Set a timer. Try it for a few days and tell yourself you're going to invest in your relationship with God for a set amount of time. This might sound strange, like you're forcing Jesus into a time slot, but if it helps you stay focused, I don't think He minds. He's overjoyed that we want to focus on Him completely for even a few minutes, and for some of us using a timer can be reassuring. It frees our thoughts from having to wander back to the clock and our busy schedules; we're free to focus on our relationship with God until the timer goes off. Here are suggestions:

- **Five or Ten Minutes**. If you're starting out, first try five, then ten minutes. Remember we're not in a race to fill some spiritual Superhero shoes. There's grace to let God into whatever space you're able to give Him, so find what works for you.
- **Twenty Minutes**: After you establish a daily habit, maybe experiment with 20 minutes. After all, we easily spend 20 minutes on social media, right? Twenty minutes with our Lord give us the time we need to make a meaningful connection with Him, hear His voice through the words of a Scripture passage, and pray a few minutes to invite Him to come into our day and touch us and our loved ones.
- **Thirty Minutes:** If 20 minutes leave you longing for more, try 30? Most days we spend 30 minutes watching the evening news or a sitcom, but we can also learn to read scripture, pray, and reflect or journal for half an hour. Setting aside more time to spend with God doesn't make us holier. It might just mean we're more desperate. Experiment to find the balance between what you need and how much time you're able to set aside and actually focus.

FINDING YOUR BEST TIME

"Very early in the morning, while it was still dark, Jesus got up, left the house and went off to a solitary place, where he prayed." (Mark 1:35)

If we think we're busy, reading the gospels reminds us that Jesus had even more on His plate than we do. His days were full of preaching, teaching, traveling, and healing. Yet Mark 1:35 reveals a touching picture of Jesus' first priority for the day. He got up early to pray, so He could start off the morning with His Father.

Productivity experts say we should complete our top priority tasks first thing and save less important jobs for later in the day. Nothing is more important to me than my daily time with God, so if I really want to make sure I do it, I fit it in first. Taking time to read Scripture and pray puts me in a more hopeful place each morning and sets the tone for the rest of my day. It also gives me a chance to ask God for wisdom and empowerment for the tasks ahead of me.

Taking time to read Scripture and pray puts me in a more hopeful place each morning.

However, Jesus also prayed at night! Mark 6, which includes the famous "walking on water" story, tells us that after Jesus preached and fed the 5,000 people, He dismissed the crowd. "After leaving them, he went up on a mountainside to pray" (Mark 6:46). Later that night, Jesus saw the disciples out on the lake straining against the oars, but He continued praying until shortly before dawn, when He finally went out to them.

Maybe you're a night person, and for you praying at night comes more naturally while praying in the morning is like climbing Mount Everest. I happen to be one of those morning people whose brain is mush by 10:00 pm, but if you're one of the lucky people who can think about more than Styrofoam at that hour, you might want to have your quiet time before bed. Go for it!

Isaiah 26:9 describes what it means to follow hard after God, morning and night: "My soul yearns for you in the night; in the morning my spirit longs for you." The hour we do it doesn't matter, but setting aside a consistent time each day does because it helps us develop a habit. The demands of life, ever-changing family schedules, and our own multi-tasking tendencies distract us to no end, but setting apart the same time each day for God helps us make quiet time part of our daily pattern. That same time everyday becomes an anchor in our lives. The commitment to meet with God each day develops an inner attitude of the heart to put Him first.

> *The commitment to meet with God each day develops an inner attitude of the heart to put Him first.*

CREATE A PLACE

Just last week a friend who struggles to spend consistent time with God told me about a fond memory she has. When she first came to Christ, she set apart a space for prayer in her house. She put out a little cross and a candle where she could see them, and she remembers how they helped her effort to enter into God's presence.

What if we set aside a special place in our homes to meet with God for prayer and Bible reading? Maybe a comfortable armchair near a window could work for you, or a desk in your bedroom, or your dining room table or living room couch. Give it a pretty detail like a vase of flowers, a lovely table cloth, or a plant. Add something that will inspire you, like a candle or stones from the beach. Make it a place you enjoy and take joy in creating it.

If you can, go back to that same spot each day, so that it signals to your mind, "Here's where I slow down my soul to meet with God." For a distracted woman like me, it's easier to quiet my thoughts and focus on Jesus when I go back to the same place each day. That might sound crazy, but it worked for my friend, and it works for me.

Right now, my place to meet with the Lord is my office. I keep colored pencils and pens, my Bible, a journal, and a few devotionals on hand, so everything's ready when I find time. Usually I'm the kind of woman who has to dig for five minutes to find a pencil in her purse, or search through the entire house for her keys before finding them in the refrigerator, so it helps me to have a place for everything (and to actually put everything in its place, but that's another story). If I keep what I'll need in my special place, I don't have to spend time each morning searching the house for my Bible. In our last home, I had a quiet time spot in the den, so I kept my supplies in a basket next to the couch. Having a place in my home works for me, but if it works better for you to meet with God in the park during your lunch hour, you might keep your Bible and supplies in a backpack.

MINIMIZE DISTRACTIONS

Because my mind easily goes off in a thousand directions at once, I have to take measures if I'm going to try to give God quality time. For me that means putting my to-do list away and ignoring my phone. It means finding a relatively calm, uncluttered spot where I can sit peacefully without stressing out and going off on an inner rant to the tune of *"How on earth have I allowed this place to get into such a mess?"*

I've also always tried to find a time when my kids were sleeping. Anyone with kids knows if they're awake, they can't wait twenty minutes without wanting to know what's for dinner or asking if you've seen their green socks. I love my kids and want to be the best mom possible, but I need a brief spiritual vacation every day, a time just for me and Jesus, so that I can receive more of His love for me and be empowered to love others well later in the day. If at all possible, I carve out a time I can actually be alone.

No matter what time and place we choose, it won't be easy to focus on our Lord and engage with His Word for 20, or even 10 minutes in this age of distraction. This probably isn't news to you since we live in the same world where social media has trained our brains to scatter thoughts in a hundred directions as we receive notifications on our phones.

After years of judging all my friends, I often find myself checking Facebook or Instagram right after I wake up. And early morning is often the best time to check in on my son, who's away at college. Some days I send him a text, and then during my quiet time, I find my hand reaching for the phone to see if he has messaged me yet. For me, finding inner stillness to hear God's quiet voice is harder than ever before.

A friend of mine who leads a youth group implements a "No phone" approach to her youth meetings. She noticed that instead of interacting with each other, giving their all in worship, or listening intently to a talk, her younger friends were scrolling down their feeds, uploading pictures to Instagram, or texting. So now she has a box at the doorway where she collects phones. After handing them over, the young people interact a lot more and remember again how to have fun talking and joking around.

What if we approach our time with Jesus the same way and leave our phone in a pretty basket in our special meeting place? My best strategy for taming the media monster in my life is to turn my phone to silent and leave it on the other side of the room. I actually do use it often to read a devotional app I like or to look up Bible verses, so it takes extra discipline to put it back in its place when I'm done.

WHAT IF IT DOESN'T CHANGE MY DAY?

What if you're trying to give God your all during that time, but your face falls flat into your Bible, your eyes glaze over, and you zone out? It happens to me all the time. What if you have a whole week of those days? Friend, you're not alone.

Some mornings during my quiet time, I feel God right there in the room speaking to me. I receive a special word I need to make it through my day or the encouragement I need for a problem I'm facing. Other days, my mind wanders to the moon and back as I fight boredom or drowsiness.

So what do you do when it seems like day after day you show up, but there aren't any fireworks? No words from God. Your devotional time grows duller than Dullsville. Quiet time with God is one area in my life where I've seen the value of just showing up, even when I don't feel like it. When I keep showing up, sooner or later things change. All of a sudden, I sense God coming through for me in new ways, and I become more attentive to His voice.

We never know when a mini-revival or spiritual breakthrough is going to come, but it always does. If we give up too soon, we never experience it. The important thing is to keep a space in our lives open for God, to keep opening the door and inviting Him in.

Even when our quiet time has grown dull, let's keep showing up. Spiritual renewal may be just around the corner.

Of course, there'll be many days when we just can't make it. We oversleep, or fall asleep, or keep company with a baby who never sleeps. We set our alarms and wake up, but the kids wake up too, an hour earlier than normal. One of the best secrets to meaningful connection with God is not letting the glitches derail us. We don't have to wallow in guilt over not managing to set aside time with God in the morning, and we don't have to let it ruin our day or keep us from turning our hearts to the Lord later on.

Sometimes we need to get creative. When I had babies, I often propped my Bible up on the same pillow I used to support their heads while breastfeeding. My busy friend Amy says her best prayer times are when she's in the car alone on the way to work. Driving keeps her alert, yet doesn't require so much thought that she's unable to pray. Staying awake to God throughout the day and looking for creative ways to connect with Him are more important than checking off the box that we did it for 20 minutes in the morning.

5

Finding Focus

During my childhood, our family always laughed at my grandfather's ability to be physically present, but mentally absent. Back in the day before "being present" was even a thing, Grandfather would sit in his own little world surrounded by noisy us at family gatherings. He was a gruff, crusty old Texas lawyer, and we were all secretly scared of him. But he had a heart of gold, and one of Grandfather's funniest — but little known — sides was that he loved reading Victorian romance novels. He lent me books by the bagful when I was in junior high.

One day when we went to visit my grandparents, I carried a big grocery bag of books into their living room, set it down, and said, "I finished these books, Grandfather. Thanks for lending them to me."

"You're welcome. Glad you enjoyed them," he said. We sat around the table and started talking.

Thirty minutes later, Grandfather abruptly interrupted the conversation, "Betsy, what happened to those books I lent you? Did you ever read them?"

He was completely baffled when everyone else in the room burst out laughing. We all loved him and at least theoretically knew he loved us, but establishing a close connection with him was next to impossible because he usually stayed in his own preoccupied world. His body was with us, but his mind was back at the law office.

Fast forward thirty years, and I'm not much better today than my Grandfather was back then. I inherited something of his absent-minded nature although, thankfully, I'm not quite as gruff and scary as he was. (*I don't think.*) Unless I make an effort to listen, I miss the conversation. I ask a question, and my kids say, "Mom, I just said that!" I ask my daughter what she wants for Christmas, and she says, "Mom, you asked me this yesterday." Sometimes at church or in a crowd, my husband has to say, "Betsy, did you hear that woman say hello to you?" I might be looking straight at someone, yet somehow miss that they're speaking to me.

Just as I want to be present and focus my attention on people I love around me, I also want to be present to God during the time I spend with Him. Yet many days my reality is different. I zone in and out during a devotional time that seems more like a drag than an inspiring encounter with the Lord of the universe. In the morning I pour myself some coffee and sit down with my Bible, but my mind zips to my daughter's orthodontist appointment. I remember we're out of bread and milk.

I open my Bible, read through the passage of the day, and realize five minutes later I parked my mind in La La Land while reading. I try to rally my attention back to the Lord and start reading or praying again. Five minutes later, I repeat the same sequence. I'm just not feeling it, so I check Facebook or get started on my grocery list. Does this sound familiar?

I'm learning the quality of my quiet time improves when I start out on the right foot during the first minutes. When I remember this is my precious chance to drop everything aside and draw near to my Creator, it helps me get intentional about focusing on Him. When I remind myself that this is my golden opportunity to receive guidance for my day and strength for my heart, it creates a desire to take advantage of special moments with my Savior. My quiet time with Him becomes more meaningful. Starting off with an intention to focus on God sets me up to receive more encouragement and substance in the time that follows.

I find more focus when I remember this is my precious chance to drop everything aside and draw near to my Creator.

FIRST STEP: OPEN THE DOOR TO INVITE GOD IN

A simple prayer of invitation can start our quiet time on a more powerful and purposeful note. Many days, when I sit down at my desk to spend time with Jesus, I imagine Him right in front of me, and I invite Him to sit down. When I intentionally invite my Savior to come close to me, my faith grows, and often I have a keener sense of His presence with me right there in the moment.

Other days, I imagine opening the doors of my heart and asking Christ to come in and make His home inside me. As I remember these words Paul prayed for the Ephesians, I'm encouraged to pray them for myself: "I pray that out of his glorious riches he may strengthen you with power through his Spirit in your inner being, so that Christ my dwell in your hearts through faith" (Ephesians 3:16-17). I pray that by faith His presence inside me will become real to me at that moment.

The book of James gives us a clear command and promise: "Draw near to God, and He will draw near to you" (4:8). What if we start our quiet times with a simple prayer like this: "Lord, I want to draw near to you right now. Will you come and show yourself to me? Will you speak to me during our time together?" When we call on the Lord to draw near to us, surely we delight His heart. When we ask God to show us more of Himself, we're praying a prayer He waits to hear and longs to answer. At the same time, we're starting off with an intention to shift our focus off the world and onto our Lord.

When we ask God to show us more of Himself, we're praying a prayer He waits to hear and longs to answer.

Inviting God to be present and reveal Himself to us is an important first step, but we can also use simple habits and practices to help us find focus as we start our quiet times.

SIGNALS OUR MINDS AND HEARTS NEED

Our crazy, media-saturated world trains our thoughts to flit from one thing to the next, and our own responsibilities and challenges sometimes make our hearts race. Yet we can also learn to still our minds and hearts before the Lord. Pausing a moment to invite God to quiet our hearts and fill them with His Holy Spirit helps us find stillness. For me, starting my quiet time with a concrete practice also helps me find focus. A few simple habits and spiritual routines send a signal to my distracted, over-worked, and over-tired brain that it is time to get quiet, relax, and shift my focus to God. Obviously we can't do all of these every day, but choosing one centering practice can help us enter God's presence more fully. If these don't help you, feel free to skip them.

Silence and Stillness

We don't usually think of silence as multi-sensory, but the absence of noise can speak peace to our senses. Sometimes sitting still and silent a few moments helps us gain an awareness of God with us and gives us the opportunity we need to let go of worries and thoughts of our to-do list. In the quiet, we become more attuned to God's voice.

Sit, Stand, or Kneel

My husband kneels each night to pray before he gets into bed. Once in a blue moon I actually get down on the floor to kneel myself, but not always. When I do, I find the simple act of changing my posture sends a signal to my mind and body that now is the time to draw near to my Father. Somehow kneeling helps me remember who I am and who God is. Bowing down or prostrating ourselves can help scattered brains shift gears and find awareness of God's presence.

Years ago, I joined the women at my church to go through a Beth Moore study called *Stepping Up: A Journey Through the Psalms of Ascent*.[1] In one of the teaching videos, I heard Beth say she went through a time where she started each day flat on her face, asking God's Spirit to come and fill her. A friend in our study group joked about how she herself couldn't prostrate herself in her living room because she was afraid of what she'd see or smell in the carpet under her face, but I tried it a few times. It reminded me that any ground can become holy ground when we're aware of God's presence.

Songs

One of my favorite ways to slip into God's presence at the start of my quiet time is to listen to a song. In fact, my kids almost roll their eyes when they hear the song "Good Good Father" because they heard strains of it coming from the living room every morning the summer before last. It pulled me through during a difficult period when my mother-in-law passed away and my husband went to his home country for three weeks. I'd listen to it, and God would pour strength into me as I sang, "You are perfect in all of your ways."[2] Six months later, during a six-week marathon of medical testing, I listened to "Great Are You Lord" every day. Singing out loud, "It's your breath in our lungs," I'd stand and pray for healing, health, and all the other prayer requests a woman on her last leg can think of.[3]

Singing a quiet song ourselves can be an even better way to open our hearts to the God who is near. I have a few default songs I sometimes sing when I want to recognize God with me during a quiet moment at home or in the car. My favorite is a brief song about God's love. When I sing it and ask the Lord to pour his love over me, He never fails to bless me with a heightened awareness of His presence with me and His care for me.

A Candle

While I write this, it's a blistering July day, and a fan provides my only relief from the heat. Yet I have a candle burning next to me. Call me crazy, but even on a summer day, lighting a candle gives me a visual reminder of God's presence. It awakens in me a heightened awareness of the Holy Spirit. The action of lighting it in the morning sends a signal to my spirit: God is here, and this is a special time for praying and listening to Him. I love lavender, vanilla, and seasonal scents, and their fragrance reminds me the Holy Spirit is with me. During the years when I home-schooled my kids, I'd leave my quiet time candle burning for the rest of the morning as a special reminder of God's

Spirit all around us and in us. It kept me sane on many chaotic mornings with the kids.

ENGAGING OUR MINDS

Concrete, multi-sensory signals help me turn my attention away from the demands of my day and towards God, but if I don't engage my mind quickly, I zone out again fast. Because I have the attention span of a five-year-old. Although some days maybe my soul needs to sit still, daydream or just be, generally I want my quiet time to be a small window in my day for seeking to hear from God. To keep from spacing out, I need to intentionally focus my thoughts. These activities get my mind warmed up before I open my Bible to seek to hear God's voice. Again, these are ideas to choose from, not a "check off the box" list. Some days I do one, two, or none of these.

Review

Looking back at what I read the day before, noticing any verses I highlighted or any note I jotted down, gives me a sense of continuity from day to day. Reviewing what I felt God spoke to me the day before is a great way to get myself in a frame of mind to hear His voice today. It adds meaning and continuity to my devotional life as I look for common threads in what God is showing me.

If you use a spiritual journal, take a moment every few days to look back over recent entries. Did you copy a verse or write out a prayer? You just might find the surprise of realizing God actually answered a prayer you'd forgotten about. Perhaps a promise you jotted down a few days ago speaks to your situation today as well.

Read a Psalm

Most days I begin my quiet time by reading a Psalm. I like to read it out loud, or at least in a whisper if other members of my family are already milling about the house. Reading aloud helps me feel like I'm praying the words for myself. In the Psalms, I discover words for every situation: for times when I'm afraid, hurt, angry, sad, depressed, lost, facing challenges, or feeling happy. I find Psalms of lament, doubt, thanks, and praise. After reading a Psalm almost every day for 30 years, I've discovered that when I face a personal trial, I can almost always think of a Psalm that speaks to my situation. In fact, I have a friend who teases me, saying Psalms are all I read and know, but I don't care. They work for me, helping me relate to God.

Praise and Thanks

Praise and thanksgiving are keys that open a door to God's presence. Psalm 100:4 says it well: *"Enter his gates with thanksgiving and his courts with praise; give thanks to him and praise his name."* No matter what challenges we're going through, or how bleak the day looks when we wake up, a few moments of mindful thanksgiving for God's blessing can turn our outlook around. Praise helps us remember God is greater than any giant we're facing right now; it reminds us that God will show Himself faithful and we can trust His love for us.

Praise helps us remember God is greater than any giant we're facing right now.

Repent

We kind of hate the word "repentance" because who wants to be reminded of what they've done wrong? I easily forget I'm the sinner Jesus died for, and I can go days without even remembering my sins, much less repenting from them. Without realizing it, I fall into the "I'm a good person" mindset. However, I've discovered that taking time to call my sins to mind and ask God for forgiveness opens my life up to renewal and frees me to enter into a deeper relationship with my Lord and receive more of His grace. It puts me on the right footing to enter His presence.

A few moments of prayerful repentance after reading these verses works wonders for my soul:

"Search me, O God, and know my heart;
Try me and know my anxious thoughts;
And see if there be any hurtful way in me,
And lead me in the everlasting way."
Psalm 139:23, 24 (NASB)

Read a favorite Devotional

Because my brain starts working slowly in the morning, reading a devotional can gently get it moving towards God. Some days I sit down to read one of my favorites while I wait for my coffee maker to brew its morning magic. I like Proverbs 31 Ministries' *First5* phone app and *Jesus Calling* by Sarah Young. I've also used devotionals by favorite authors, like Suzie Eller's *Come with Me Devotional*. When sitting down to read a full-length Christian book is harder to fit into my schedule, I can receive mini-bites of spiritual encouragement and wisdom through reading devotionals.

Review Scripture Memory Verses

Re-reading old memory verses is also a good way to pass a few morning minutes while I wait for coffee in the kitchen. Repeating them gets me into a frame of mind to connect with God through His Word during my quiet time. I have a little green book I've used for years to write Scripture memory verses in. On days when I actually know where my little green book is, I use it to review Scripture I've memorized.

Another way I get my scattered brain moving in God's direction is to actually learn a new verse written on an index card. (For me, an index card is the ultimate on-the-go tool that always gets lost, but I use it until it disappears into the chaos of my home or car). I'm not always working on Scripture memory, but when I am, I pick up an index card each morning and repeat the verse I'm trying to learn. God shows me different things about my verse each day when I repeat it to myself, and by the end of the week, I have it memorized.

GIVING OURSELVES GRACE WHEN DISTRACTION HITS

Despite all our efforts to pay attention to God during our time with Him, distraction will keep coming at us in a thousand little ways through stray thoughts, beeps from the telephone we forgot to put into silent mode, and the feelings of exhaustion most working moms experience. It's easy to forget we're in God's presence, and we just might fritter away our time daydreaming, thinking about our to-do list, or wondering about the latest in our Instagram feed. When we struggle to stay attentive, let's give ourselves grace. After all, we're only human. Keeping our time with God fairly short can help us learn the art of paying attention, and in turn makes that time more meaningful.

For me, half the battle against distraction lies in actively engaging my mind in the right place before it wanders. This list of ways to find focus helps me deal proactively with my wandering thoughts. Doing one or two of them as I start my quiet time puts me in a more attentive frame of mind. I also like to change things up. Novelty somehow motivates me and holds my attention, so I read a Psalm aloud one day, start with a memory verse the next, and light a candle or try to sit still and quiet the next. Changing these keeps me from falling into a rut, and doing something proactive to engage my mind helps me intentionally enter God's presence before I turn to read Scripture and seek to hear His voice.

6

Getting Goodness from God's Word

Have you ever turned on a water faucet, but nothing came out? Back when my husband and I were newly married and living in El Salvador, our neighborhood had running water only one hour a day. And that hour happened to start at 3:00 a.m.!

We'd set an alarm before going to bed every night, and believe it or not, when that alarm sounded at 3:00, I'd jump out of bed to start the washing machine while José filled plastic storage containers in the bathrooms. Making sure to turn on the washing machine first thing guaranteed that an entire wash cycle could finish before the water cut off. Filling the storage container in the shower meant we could bathe the next day, and I won't go into the reason behind the containers next to the toilets, but you can probably guess. Then we'd wash any stray dishes in the kitchen and fill the large reservoir sink on the patio before falling back into bed.

It only took a month for us to realize we couldn't live that way. Sleep deprivation, inconvenience, plus a thriving mosquito population due to standing water around the house in our tropical country all worked together to force us to have a tank built in our backyard. That meant the tank would fill up each night while we slept, and the following day water would flow like normal from the taps.

We take water for granted until we don't have any. Tasks like doing laundry, washing dishes, and other unmentionables become impossible without it. Most importantly, we need water to quench our thirst and stay healthy. Can you imagine going through a day without one sip of water? You'd end up with a big headache and no energy.

We need the Word like we need water.

Doctors say we need eight glasses of water each day to stay healthy. Flowers can't grow, fish can't swim, and runners can't run marathons without water. In the same way, believers need frequent intake of God's Word. As we read it, the Holy Spirit brings it to life. Scripture feeds our faith, renews our thoughts, and empowers us to run our race. God's Word gives us hope and encouragement when we're battling doubt or depression. It imparts the wisdom we need when we don't know how to respond to the challenges of life or to that impossible person in the office next to us at work. And when we lose our way, God's Word will light our path.

Scripture feeds our faith, renews our thoughts, and empowers us to run our race.

BORED WITH THE BIBLE?

Although God has given us a powerful gift in His written Word, many of us have had less-than-exciting encounters with it. Back in my pre-teen days when I dreamed of being a nun, I carried around in my heart a secret longing to know more of God, but I didn't know what to do with it. Determined to read the Bible every day, I'd open the cracked blue leather cover of my great-grandmother's antique King James Bible. I'd start on page one: "In the beginning God created the heaven and the earth. And the earth was without form, and void; and darkness was upon the face of the deep. And the Spirit of God moved upon the face of the waters…" (Genesis 1:1-2 KJV).

By the time I got to Adam and Eve, I'd be snoozing, so I'd put the book back on the shelf. Maybe, just maybe, I'd try again on day two, but the same thing would happen. Then I'd put that Bible back and forget about it for several months before getting it down and starting with Genesis 1 all over again. My first impression of the Bible? Boring.

Now I can laugh about this, yet many days I still approach the Bible the same way. I come to God's Word like it's a textbook I've got to read to be a "good girl." My eyes glaze over as I read the same passages for the hundredth time without thinking. I forget what a miracle and awesome treasure I have at my fingertips.

The very same God who breathed life into the universe breathed words into the hearts of men: sojourners, shepherds, slaves, kings, singers, priests, fishermen, and even a doctor. Over a period of 2,000 years, they recorded the words we hold in our hands today, words that point to a loving God who created our world and redeemed it from sin by sending His son to die. When we read Scripture, God's Spirit breathes life into it, and it comes to life inside us. It changes our hearts and renews our minds. The God of the Universe wants to speak to us.

Reading God's Word has many benefits: guidance, wisdom, hope, faith, power, and transformation. All these can be ours when we read Scripture, but to receive them we must pursue them. We need to read God's Word actively, to go after truth with all our hearts. For Scripture to become meaningful, we have to mine its treasures. I love the phrase "Scripture engagement" because it reminds me to read Scripture with the goal of interacting with God. When I read His Word, I can expect to hear from the God of the Universe, and He waits for me to respond in turn. And that, my friend, is a miracle indeed.

When we read His Word, we can expect to hear the God of the universe speaking to us.

GETTING MORE GOODNESS FROM GOD'S WORD

If you, like me, want to get more out of God's Word when you read it, the ideas I share in the following section and in the next chapter may help. If you'd like tips on how to understand God's Word better, have a closer connection with Him while you read, and actually apply it to your life, read on!

Word for Today

If you read nothing else in this book, I'd want to tell you about my "Word for Today" method. I also like to call it spiritual journaling for the busy and distracted, and I'm sharing it first because it breathes fresh air into my Bible reading.

This may sound crazy, but I love choosing one word for the day from my morning Scripture reading. It's the easiest way I know to take what I read with me into the rest of my day. I learned it from a dear, elder sister in the faith during a prayer retreat. Rather than a serious Bible study method, it's a way to seek to hear God's voice through the words of Scripture. This may be a bit out of the box for you, and if you're spooked because you think I'm getting overly spiritual on you, then skip it. But it works for me, and here's how to do it:

- Read the passage once quickly, and then a second time prayerfully and slowly.
- Choose one verse that speaks to you the most. Write your verse down, and read it several times

slowly, asking God to show you one word that sums it up best.

- Write your word down. Spend a few moments thinking and praying. What does the word mean to you and how it might make a difference in your day? Ask God if He wants to speak anything to you through your word. Be still and actually listen for a few moments. Do any impressions come to mind?

- If you like, write a one sentence prayer in response to what God showed you. Make an intention to remember your word and your prayer later during the day. If you forget, don't sweat it. You'll see it tomorrow in your journal.

I realize this might sound strange. Just to give you some examples, I've chosen words like "Believe," "Love," "Blessed," "Cling," "Trust," and "Hope." One word can sum up what I feel God speak to me in the morning, and I can easily remember it later in the day. In fact, I've gotten through many rough days by clinging to truth expressed in one word and turning it into a prayer. If you are looking for some fresh air in your quiet time, you might try it too.

Read, Reflect, and Respond

In her book *Pray Deep*, my friend Kathryn Shirey outlines a process of Scripture engagement: Read, Reflect, and Respond.[1] Although my approach differs from hers, I love alliteration, and those three R's help me understand the process of interacting with God's Word. I read it, reflect on what it means for my life while I seek to hear what God is saying, and finally I respond in prayer or action. I might need to take a concrete step of obedience, whether it's writing out a prayer I want to remember, jotting down a reminder to call a friend, or reaching out to apologize to someone for something God brought to my mind.

Of course, only on good days do I get to all three steps: read, reflect, and respond. Life happens, and some days I get stuck in the "read" step, but even just reading is so much better than never getting around to it. Let's take a look at how to do these three steps more effectively.

WAYS TO READ SCRIPTURE

Even just reading the Bible can seem daunting on those days when you're low on sleep and high on stress, thinking about all you have to do. Staying focused can be a challenge, especially in our information-saturated society. One reader, Holly, says this:

"I'll start reading my devotional and suddenly notice a crooked picture across the room and feel compelled to fix it. Then I'm off on an accidental bunny trail fixing this or that. Lastly, and I'm so ashamed to admit this, but I've gotten into the awful habit of scrolling through Facebook before having my devotions. And I'm a pastor's wife too. Sheesh! I'm working on that habit, but the struggle is real."[2]

I can totally understand Holly; I'm another pastor's wife who falls into the Facebook pit many days before I ever open my Bible in the morning.

Use a Plan

A Bible reading plan helps me stay focused and makes it easier to open my Bible each day because I know exactly what page to turn to without having to think about it. Whereas a random approach to flipping through Scripture gives me scattered tidbits of wisdom and encouragement, a plan helps me see a continuation of God's truth unfolding. That plan can be as simple as reading through the whole Bible, or the New Testament, or one book of the Bible.

Your Bible may have a reading plan in the back, and online sources like Bible Gateway or Navigators.org also offer them. Proverbs 31 Ministries' First 5 app offers daily devotionals written by well-known Christian writers to go along with its book-by-book reading plan. You'll learn more, stay focused, and see a progression in Scripture when you use a plan.

Read Less

Although this might sound crazy or counter-intuitive, what helps me get more out of reading Scripture is to read less. Nothing sets my mind into snooze mode more quickly than trying to plow through a "Read Your Bible in One Year" program. (*Is it okay to actually say that?*) I think it's a wonderful idea to get the whole scope of Scripture by reading it through once a year, and I respect people who do it. But I personally can't handle it because it makes my eyes glaze over.

For me to get more goodness out of God's Word, I have to read less. So I stick to reading one chapter a day, but typically I focus on a few verses or a shorter section after reading the whole chapter first. In fact for years, I read only one or two sub-titled sections each day, aiming at a total of 10-15 verses. For example, Luke 1 is broken up into seven sections with subtitles, so I'd read it over five days or so. Reading less helps me pay attention more. It helps me focus on listening for what God might be saying to me today through His Word.

Sometimes reading less helps me pay attention more to what God is saying to me through Scripture.

Read Out Loud or Listen

Actually hearing Scripture spoken brings it to life for me. Reading aloud or listening to a passage helps my mind stay engaged, especially on days when my people are busy buzzing around the house making noises that distract me. Other days, my own thoughts are busy with my to-do list or my inner rant over what's bothering me about my life right now, so reading aloud helps calm those thoughts and center them on the truth I want to absorb. Listening to audio versions of the Bible adds a new dimension as I read along.

When I pushed through the book of Numbers last year, some mornings it was hard going. Listening somehow helped me grasp that Numbers was a real history book about real people and events that really happened. I'm not sure why listening made such a big difference, but it encouraged my faith.

Read Twice

Reading a passage twice helps me dig deeper and get more out of it, which is also why I stick to shorter passages. Often, I listen first and then read silently myself. A second reading helps me notice details I miss the first time, especially when a passage seems dull or boring at first glance. As for the times when I'm reading something, and truth jumps out at me from all over the page in the form of verses and thoughts that grab my attention, reading twice helps me narrow in on one truth I want to remember for the rest of my day. It helps me to reflect on what the passage means to me personally.

REFLECT ON WHAT YOU READ

Of course, reading Scripture won't impact our lives if we don't think about what we're reading. For me, it'll just go in one ear and out the other because I have a short memory. Ask my kids. Unless I get intentional about remembering something, I forget it. I don't want to read the Bible each day just to say I did it. Instead, I want to interact with the God who loves me and longs to direct my path. Through His written Word, I hear God speak to me. Remembering this helps me keep one question at the forefront of my mind as I read Scripture: "Lord, what do you want to say to me today?"

When we read Scripture, let's ask, "Lord, what do you want to say to me today?

Ask Yourself Questions

It's so simple, but asking ourselves questions, especially as we read a passage for the second time, will help us avoid mindless skimming, so we can actually get something out of it. We might sense God's Spirit speaking as we answer questions like these:

- What does this tell me about God the Father, the Son, or the Holy Spirit?
- What difference does this make in my life today?
- Do I need to do something? What can I obey?
- What promise can I claim?
- What encouragement do I find?
- What verse speaks to me most today?

Mark it up and Make it Yours

Have you ever noticed how something about writing in a book makes it yours? Any book becomes more personal when you underline parts you like or make notes in the margin. The Bible is no different. Circling important or repeated words helps us get more out of reading it. When we make a connection between our daily lives and what we're reading, jotting down a quick note in the margin of our Bible helps us remember it later and leaves a record for the future.

Just last week, I found some notes penned in the margin of my Bible that reminded me of urgent prayer requests during a low point in my faith life two years ago. Psalm 79:8 says, "May your mercy come quickly to meet us, for we are in desperate need," and next to it I saw a brief note: "My prayer. August 2016." It reminded me of a time I felt desperate but had no idea how God would come through for me and my family. Looking back now, I can see many ways God answered that prayer and met our needs. It strengthens my faith for whatever challenges might lie ahead.

Highlighting meaningful verses in different colors not only helps us think while we read, it also leaves a record of what spoke to us for when we read that passage again in the future. When I have time, I take highlighting a step further: I like to color code different words or phrases according to the theme or meaning. It helps me get more out of a passage, and I love the way it looks later on the pages of my Bible.

Here's the system I use:

Purple: God the Father
Red: Jesus, Love
Yellow: Holy Spirit, Attributes of God, God's Kingdom
Dark Blue: Actions of God, Jesus, and the Holy Spirit
Light Blue: Faith, Hope, God's Gifts and Blessings
Dark Green: Worship, Praise, Thanks, and Joy
Light Green: People and their Characteristics

Orange: Commands
Brown: Sin
Pink: Prayer, Promises of God

RESPOND TO GOD

To be honest, many days I forget all about what I read. I feel inspired in the morning by some encouraging tidbit of truth, but I don't really respond. I jump up from my quiet time, thinking "Check you later, Jesus," and make a dash for the shower. Then by 9:00 a.m., I'm snapping at one of my kids for leaving a mess of sticky crumbs all over the kitchen table, or I'm stewing over something a friend said or didn't say.

Maybe I easily forget the truth that encouraged me because I didn't take time to react to it. Two ways that help me respond to God's Word and take it with me into my day are to pray about it and to write something down.

When we let the words we read shape our prayers, God often answers those prayers by changing us. The changes He works are often barely perceptible, but they're changes nevertheless. Thinking over questions like these as we read Scripture can guide our prayers:

- What do I need to repent from?
- What character quality can I ask God to work in me?
- Do I see something in this passage that sparks me to pray for someone else?
- How can I pray for my day? What step do I need to take?

Praying Scripture unleashes God's power over our day.

You may not be a compulsive writer-downer like I am, but jotting down even a quick note or Bible verse helps me retain what I read. Something about keeping my hands active helps my brain stay engaged. I'm much more likely to remember something later if I write it down, whether it's a prayer request or a Bible verse. Often the act of writing adds focus to my prayer, and it leaves me a record to look at later as well.

In this chapter, I've talked about several ways we can get more encouragement for our faith out of God's Word as we read it. I've shared my favorite "Word for Today" method as well as ideas about reading, reflecting on and responding to Scripture, but I don't mean to suggest we should put all these together into a quiet time format for every day. That would take two hours instead of 20 minutes! Instead, I'm suggesting different ideas to pick and choose from, using what works for you.

If you're like me, you might find that alternating methods once in a while will bring freshness and renewal to your quiet time. The ideas I've shared help me with daily devotional reading, which has been a life-transforming practice in my journey with Jesus over 35 years. Even ten minutes of reading with a prayerful attitude makes such a big difference in our lives, but sometimes we need to dig a little deeper and do purposeful study. In the next chapter, you'll find some ideas busy women can use for better Bible study.

7

Simple Study Ideas for Busy Women

My sweet mother-in-law was still a spring chicken at age 89. Almost crippled by arthritis in her knees, she could barely walk, but she could crack jokes with the best of them. She'd throw back her head and laugh loud, and she didn't let any doctor stop her enjoyment of *café con pan dulce*. (Coffee and cake are a serious Salvadoran institution.)

Mama Ofelia was not about to let difficulty walking keep her at home, and my sister-in-law drove her where she wanted to go. Always sporting a nice dress and beautiful makeup, she'd hobble out the door all the way to the car with a cane, which she'd leave in the driveway so no one would see it. Nothing kept her from her weekly trip to the beauty shop, and she'd always be ready to go out for coffee. And Bible study. She never missed it if she could help it.

At age 89, Mama Ofe graduated from a Bible Leadership Institute. She could have thought, "What's the use? I'm too old for this." But Ofelia wanted to grow, so she had enrolled in a two-year Bible program at age 87. I'm sure she enjoyed the company of her classmates, but she also knew that God's Word equips us with what we need for life. At any age and stage.

Ofelia died peacefully at 90, certain she was going straight to the presence of Jesus. When she passed out of this world, we grieved and celebrated. We knew the angels were setting off fireworks in heaven, and we gave tearful thanks for her precious legacy of faithfulness to God and treasuring His word. I hope to be like her.

I figure if an 89-year-old lady almost crippled with arthritis could hobble around to get herself to Bible study, I can make an effort to study God's Word too.

We may not be able to devote as much time to studying the Bible as my mother-in-law, but no matter our life stage, we gain a hundred-fold from any small efforts we make to study and meditate on Scripture. A mom of small children may not have the luxury of attending a Bible study course, but she can grab 10-15 minutes while babies sleep or kids watch a video. Maybe a working mom has no opportunity to attend a morning ladies' Bible study and no energy to even crack open her Bible by evening, but she can set aside a few minutes during her lunch hour once a week. Perhaps one simple secret to getting around to Bible study is to let go of perfectionism.

WE MAKE BIBLE STUDY TOO HARD

We make Bible study more complicated than it has to be. Often, we take an "all or nothing" approach to studying

Scripture, and we assume we need to lug out the concordances, Bible dictionaries, and commentaries. Of course, to get anything out of it, we have to take pages of notes, and who has time for that? It looks overwhelming, so we never get around to it.

But Bible study doesn't have to be rocket science. In fact, we don't even really *have* to do it; daily devotional reading is probably more important for deepening our relationship with God. We find so much benefit through simply reading Scripture, asking God to speak to us, and then responding to Him through prayer. However, simple Bible study can help us along our journey to more of God by giving us more insight into His Word and how we can live it out. It doesn't have to be long and complicated. Taking ten or fifteen minutes once or twice a week to do a bit of simple Bible study develops our faith and helps us grow deeper roots into God's truth and love.

Consider these ideas if you want to dig deeper into the Bible, but if you're struggling just to develop a daily reading habit, feel free to skip these for now and go to the next chapter, where we'll talk about ways we can get more enjoyment out of our time with God.

WHEN YOU HAVE FIVE MINUTES

I don't mean to be flippant or suggest a quick-fix, microwave-fast approach to Bible study. Of course, it's worth putting more time into it, but sometimes five minutes is all we have to spare. It may be five minutes tacked to the end of our quiet time, or five minutes we grab later in the day. Maybe five minutes will turn into ten, but it's easier to say, "I'll sit down for five minutes now to look more deeply into God's Word" than to wonder, "How can I carve an hour out of my schedule today?" God is pleased by even the smallest steps we make towards Him.

God is pleased by even the smallest steps we make towards Him.

Compare Different Versions of Scripture

Choose a verse or brief passage to read in several different versions of Scripture. Use your phone to easily access several versions at the same time, using an app like YouVersion (my personal favorite). It only takes a few minutes, but I love the insight that comes through this simple study technique:

> "You make known to me the path of life; in your presence there is fullness of joy." Psalm 16:11a (ESV)
>
> "You make known to me the path of life; you will fill me with joy in your presence." (NIV)
>
> "You have shown me the path to life, and you make me glad by being near to me." (CEV)
>
> "You will show me the way of life, granting me the joy of your presence." (NLT)
>
> "You will show me the path of life; In Your presence is fullness of joy." (NKJV)

Look up Related Verses

Choose a concept, word, or theme that stood out to you in your reading time and look up related verses. Use Google or the search feature on a Bible app or website like Biblestudytools.com. If you prefer to get away from technology during your Bible study time, you can also look at the old-fashioned cross references found for each verse right there on the pages of any good study Bible. Do what works best for you.

For example, a quick search for the phrase "living water" yields these verses:

"My people have committed two sins: They have forsaken me, the spring of living water, and have dug their own cisterns, broken cisterns that cannot hold water." (Jeremiah 2:13)

"Whoever believes in me, as Scripture has said, rivers of living water will flow from within them." (John 7:38)

"For the Lamb at the center of the throne will be their shepherd; 'he will lead them to springs of living water.' 'And God will wipe away every tear from their eyes.'" (Revelation 7:17)

Memorize a Verse

Memorizing Scripture may not be Bible study, but it could be the most life-changing way to engage with God's Word and meditate on it. Memorizing helps us fix God's words in our minds and write them on our hearts. Perhaps there's no better way to spend five minutes than to write down a verse, read it aloud ten times, and then try saying it from memory five times.

If you make note of verses or words that interest you during your quiet time, you'll have something ready to dive into when you find a few minutes for Scripture study or meditation. Highlight those verses in your Bible or write them in a notebook, so that when you find time later, you'll have something to look at when you want to compare translations, look up related verses, or commit Scripture to memory.

WHEN YOU HAVE FIFTEEN MINUTES

Try Verse Mapping

Verse mapping is one of my favorite ways to dig deeper into God's Word because it puts a fun, creative spin on Bible study. I like to think of it as making my own personal map of a Bible verse. This technique can help you mine more truth and application ideas out of your favorite verses.

It can also inspire you on those days when you read your Bible and think, "What? What does this have to do with me?" Maybe you're reading an Old Testament passage, and you just don't get it. Or you're skimming over something you've read a hundred times thinking, *"Been here. Read before."* If you're like me, you wonder if you should stick with it or just ditch your quiet time.

Just to show you the reality of my own Bible reading experience, I was definitely considering skipping out one day while reading Joshua 3, the story of the Israelites getting ready to cross the Jordan. It's an amazing story, but I was getting nothing out of it. Even all the highlighting

I'd done the previous year gave me zero encouragement for my life that particular day.

Finally, a nugget of truth in verse 5 caught my attention: *"Consecrate yourselves, for tomorrow the Lord will do amazing things among you."* I could see the verse had a command and a promise. But what did that word "consecrate" mean? I figured "consecrate yourselves" was something more for priests and Old Testament people than for home schooling moms.

I wrote it down anyway and decided to do some verse mapping. As I looked up different translations, I saw that consecrating myself meant to set myself apart for God's special purposes, to prepare and purify myself, so I could be holy and useful to Him.

What I learned challenged me to think about how to consecrate myself for serving God on a daily basis: through confession of sin, prayer, worship, and seeking to equip and train myself. After 15 minutes, I was surprised by how much God spoke to me through one little verse.

Give verse mapping a try, and He'll speak to you too. Just remember there's no right or wrong way to do it. The ideas that follow will help you get started, but you don't have to use all of them for your first verse map. Start out with a few.

WHAT YOU NEED:

- Bible
- Paper. Unlined paper makes a more visually appealing verse map, but any paper, including a page from your journal, will do.

- Pens in a few colors. You might like to use a highlighter or colored pencils as well.
- Your phone. Here's one instance where your phone can actually be a blessing to your Bible study rather than a distraction!

WHAT TO DO:

- Write your verse in the center of a blank page, leaving plenty of space between the lines and in the margins. Do one or more of the following:
- With different colors, circle, box, or underline words that stand out.
- Highlight different words.
- Personalize it by writing in your name above names of Bible characters mentioned or pronouns like "he," "she," or "you."
- Add to your map by making notes in color around the margins of the page.

First read your verse in 5-10 different versions or translations of the Bible. Using your phone, enter it into the search box at BibleGateway.com, and you have the option to look at it in all English versions. The YouVersion Bible App also has a helpful "Compare" feature on their menu when you click on a verse, but you have to choose for yourself the translations you want to see.

In the margins of your map, note down different renderings of key words that add to your understanding. You can make notes in the same colors you used to circle or box the words or phrases, drawing arrows from the words to related notes in the margins. From there you can continue making additional notes in color around the page based on one or more elements you choose from these ideas:

- Use a dictionary to write down the meaning of one of your key words.
- Cross reference your verse. Using the word search feature on a Bible app or cross references in a study Bible, look for verses that have the same key word or concept and include one on your map.
- Jot down a few brainstorm ideas about how to apply this verse to your life.
- If you find a different translation of the verse that especially encourages you, write it out in a different color at the bottom of the page.

Create a personal map of your verse using colors and elements that appeal to you. Don't feel like you must include everything in your map. Simple and done in fifteen minutes is better than waiting for that day when you finally have enough time to sit down and craft the perfect verse map.

Simple and done in 15 minutes is better than waiting for that day when you might have more time.

MORE BIBLE STUDY IDEAS

So far in this chapter, we've covered ideas for doing a little Bible study to learn more about something we read in our daily quiet time. The ideas that follow go beyond daily devotional reading and probably take longer than 15 minutes. Topical study can help us find God's truth to meet our needs and equip us for life challenges. Character and book studies help us explore our particular interests and can also speak to situations we face.

Since these methods probably take longer than 15 minutes, they might venture into the realm of "Intimidating Bible Study You Never Find Time For." If these seem intimidating to you, try breaking them down into 20-minute chunks that you do in several sittings. Take a week to focus on a topic or character. Consider breaking from your regular reading plan—lightning won't strike you—to focus on Scripture that meets your particular situation or need. If finding extra time for Bible study is hard, try doing these during your quiet time. Book study, especially, works well during your quiet time over several days or weeks.

Focus on a Topic or Word.

Choose a topic that interests you or speaks to your need and spend a few minutes learning what the Bible says about it. Themes I return to again and again are God's love, joy, peace, and hope. Perhaps you want to learn more about trusting God or walking by faith. Maybe you're struggling with fear, anxiety or worry and want to find verses to help you handle your emotions. Moms struggling not to lose it when their kids drive them crazy might benefit from looking at patience or self-control.

- Look at the definition of your word in a Bible dictionary.
- Look up verses related to your chosen topic and write down a few you find particularly helpful or encouraging.
- Make a note of common threads or themes in the verses you find.
- Jot down ideas you need to put to work in your own life.
- Choose one verse you want to memorize.

Study a Bible Character.

The Bible is full of people and stories we can learn from! Choose one of the many Bible characters found on the pages of Scripture: Abraham, Jacob, Joseph, Moses, Joshua, Caleb, Ruth, Esther, David, Solomon, Mary, Peter, Paul, and others. Using either an online source or the reference section of a study Bible, make a list of major passages where this person appears. As you read them, ask yourself the following questions:

- What characteristics describe this person?
- What circumstances shaped him or her?
- How would I describe his or her relationship with God? With people?
- What can I learn from this person? How can I follow his/her example?
- What faults, or things to avoid, do I see?

Book Study

Focusing on a book helps us dig deeper to discover more of its spiritual truth and relevance for our lives. In trying this method for the first time, choose a shorter book instead of tackling a long one. Tucked in your Bible between Ephesians and Hebrews come several shorter books, starting with Philippians, Colossians, and 1 Thessalonians. Short books from the Old Testament to consider are Ruth and Jonah; since they are stories, they might be easier to take on than short prophetic books like Haggai or Nahum.

Start by reading the book through in one sitting to get a feel for its message as a whole. Try reading it just as you would any other book. You might even read it through several times, once each day.

Look for background information. First try to glean what you can from clues in the book itself, often found in the opening or closing verses. You can also use study resources to complete your research. The traditional 5 W's can guide you:

- **Who?** Who wrote the book? To whom did they write it? Who is mentioned in the book?
- **What?** What is the book about? Can you summarize it in 1-3 sentences?
- **When?** When was it written?
- **Where?** Where did the events in the book take place? Where was the author? If he wrote the book to a specific audience, where were the recipients?
- **Why?** Why was the book written? (Don't worry if you can't answer this upon first reading. John and

Luke actually tell us why they wrote, but sometimes we may have to infer as we read.)

During your reading, look for main themes. Repeated words and phrases provide good clues to the main ideas of the book. If you like this sort of thing, make an outline of the book's main points.

Next, slow down and read the book chapter by chapter, or section by section, over several days.

- Write a one-sentence summary for each chapter or section.
- Choose one or two verses that stand out to you from each chapter.
- What can you put into practice in your own life?

Let's Not Forget our Why.

When we take an active approach and dig into scripture, we absorb more of its life-giving truth. Even a bit of study can help us unpack more of the Bible, but our main goal isn't more knowledge of Scripture.

We want more of God in our lives through understanding more of His Word. We want to know Him better, and we want more of His life-giving Word in our hearts so we can live by it.

Understanding more of God's Word leads to more of Him in our lives.

But in case you think I'm getting all serious on you talking about Bible study, let's move on and look next at ways to get more enjoyment from spending time with God.

8

Making It Enjoyable

Can I be honest with you? Sometimes my quiet time seems more like a duty than a delight. Reading the Bible becomes one more thing on the list of Good Christian Girl Duties. I'm even secretly relieved when I finally finish, so I can check off that box and go on my way, either to do something more fun or else to get on with the tasks in front of me.

Duty quickly turns into Dullsville. If I don't look for ways to keep it fresh and enjoyable, my quiet time falls into stale routines before I know it. Does it happen to you too? To be honest, sometimes I show up just for the sake of saying I did it. Don't get me wrong. I believe there's important value even in just showing up, but what I really want for my quiet time is to sense more of God's presence and hear more of His voice. I want my morning time with my Lord to make a significant difference for my life later on in the day, but it's hard to find significance in something that's become mundane.

While writing this book, I asked friends on Facebook, "What's more important to you, *meaningful* time with

God or *enjoyable* time with Him?" While most people said they wanted their time with God to be meaningful, several hit upon something I'd never thought of: for our quiet time to be meaningful, it has to be enjoyable. Women of all ages said similar things:

"I need less pressure and more joy." Katie, mom of 2 school-aged kids.

"If I enjoyed my time with God more, I would spend more time there, right? I think women don't think there's much enjoyment in reading God's Word." Carmen, mom to young adult kids.

"To be meaningful and have some relevance and impact on my life, I would prefer if it could possibly be enjoyable!" Elizabeth, retired nurse and grandmother.[1]

God is not boring, and He's not a killjoy who always wants us to approach Him with somber, dutiful spirits. Scripture shows us that joy and gladness are part of His character, and God's special delight is His people: "The Lord *delights* in those who fear him, who put their hope in his unfailing love" (Psalm 147:11). As we seek to love and follow Him, we have this promise: "The Lord your God is with you, the Mighty Warrior who saves. He will take great *delight* in you..." (Zephaniah 3:17). God takes delight in us, and surely He wants us to take joy in being with Him.

God delights in us, and surely He wants us to enjoy being with Him.

When God created us in His image, He gave us the ability to enjoy and appreciate beauty and goodness. He must long for us to find gladness in Him, and He promises special blessings to those who delight in His Word. Psalm 1 reminds us, "Blessed is the one...whose *delight* is in the law of the Lord, and who meditates on his law day and night" (Psalm 1:1a, 2). God will make that person like a well-watered, fruitful tree. In Psalm 119, the Psalmist says this about God's Word: "I *delight* in your commands because I love them" (v. 47).

In Christ, we have reasons to rejoice. He has saved us from sin and given us new life. Isaiah reminds us: "I *delight* greatly in the Lord; my soul rejoices in my God. For he has clothed me with garments of salvation" (Isaiah 61:10a).

Since God created us with a sense of enjoyment, why not make it our goal to make Him our delight and enjoy spending time with Him? For several years, I prayed every day, "Lord help me to enjoy You and the life you're giving me today." Although I'm not exactly sure how God answered that prayer in concrete terms, I know I became more joyful over time.

We take joy in what's enjoyable to us, don't we? Why not seek to bring more delight into our time with God? We can start by praying, "Lord, help me to enjoy this time with you."

Let's explore ways to move from Dullsville to delight when we spend time with the Lord.

FIND ENJOYMENT THROUGH CHANGE

When something stays the same for too long, my distracted brain goes into boredom mode. Switching how I do things adds variety and helps me find new enjoyment in routine tasks. Not that I view my quiet time as a routine task, but it *is* something I do almost daily. When I've fallen into a rut, simple changes refresh my outlook on time with Jesus and help me hear His voice in new ways.

Changing the time and place is an easy way to freshen up stale quiet times. Maybe you've seen that early morning is no longer working because no matter how early you get up, your kids beat you to it. They're crying out for attention, and you're getting frustrated. Rather than beat your head against the wall, why not try a different time? Experiment to see what works or add spontaneity to the way you view your quiet time. Push the baby's stroller out the door and head to the park to pray for a few minutes. Leave for work ten minutes early, so you can sit at your desk or in the car after you arrive and read Scripture. Try fitting in a few moments of quiet after lunch or before bed.

Move your quiet time to another room in your house, or even better yet, out to the backyard or front porch if the weather permits. Sounds like singing birds and wind rushing through the trees bring joy to the soul and might even help you connect with the Maker of heaven and earth. Read Scripture and take a walk around the block while you pray, or leave traditional Bible reading aside for a day or two and take your audio Bible or worship music with you to the walking trail. In the summer I enjoy sitting out on our balcony, but even moving from the living room to the kitchen gives a different feel to my time with God.

We find new freedom and joy when we let go of what's grown stale and open the windows to fresh ways of connecting with God. A new devotional can give us fresh insights into God's truth. Starting a new reading plan can spark our love for God's Word in a different way. Experiment with a new-to-you Bible study or journaling tip. Write a letter to God, telling Him what's on your heart. I like keeping my quiet time fresh and new by opening my doors to change.

> *We find new joy when we open the windows to fresh ways of connecting with God.*

OPEN THE DOOR TO CREATIVITY

A little creativity can go a long way to add fun or inspiration to our time with God. You may think you don't have a creative bone in your body, but I bet you do. As a kid, I remember my mother praising my brother's artistic abilities, and for years I thought I wasn't creative because I couldn't draw like he did. Later I realized how much I enjoy needlework, flower arranging, cooking new foods, creating with paper, and crafting a pretty or powerful phrase with words. I enjoy trying new things and thinking up novel ways to do something. I bet you have your own brand of artistry as well. We can put our creativity to work experimenting with new ways to relate to God and respond to His Word.

Unlike me, maybe you enjoy or have a knack for drawing. Have you ever thought about drawing a picture in response to something you discovered in your Bible reading? I couldn't draw to save my life, but I don't let it stop me from doodling hearts, flowers, and a few sometimes-unrecognizable objects in my journal. Break out the colored pencils and pens. Choose a word for the day like we talked about using the Word for Today devotional method and make a small sketch to go with it. Embellish a Bible verse with a few swirls and circles when you when you write it out in your journal.

My friend Jana probably has more creativity in her little finger than I have in my whole body. Recently I attended a Bible journaling workshop she gave, and I was surprised by how much fun I had experimenting with print-outs she had created, scrapbooking paper, water colors, gelato crayons, washi tape, and lots of other mysterious materials my craft-challenged self had never seen! Jana shared that she has a journaling Bible separate from her reading Bible — another secret I didn't know — so she doesn't worry about covering up parts of her Bible pages with craft materials. She has another one for reading. When I leafed through the pages of her big, beautiful Bible, I could see Jana has a scrapbook of the verses God has used to speak to her at different seasons of her life, a beautiful record of her walk with Jesus.[2]

We think of our quiet times in terms of left-side brain functions like reading, praying, and writing, but what if we added more imaginative activities that appeal to our senses and stimulate the right side of our brain? After all, we're spending time with God, the most creative being who ever lived. So croon out a worship song. Play your instrument. Read Scripture aloud with artistic expression or listen to a dramatized reading of the Bible.

We make prayer into a purely cognitive activity, but it can also be multi-sensory. Draw, paint, or listen to a worship song as you pray. Write a few lines of a poem in response to what you sense God speaking to you. Instead of a prayer list, use a stack of photos to pray for people as you flip through the pictures. Or doodle a design or picture around someone's name as you pray for them.

Instead of a fifteen-minute Bible study time once a week, what if we gave fifteen minutes of creative time to our relationship with the Lord? Try something new. Experiment with painting, pastels, or handcrafts. Write and sing a song based on a Psalm that encourages your spirit. Make a graphic organizer or collage in response to something you read in God's Word. Pick up a cheap copy of the Bible at a thrift store, so you won't be worried about "ruining" an expensive Bible when you experiment with artistic Bible journaling or scrapbooking. Sew or make a gift for someone, praying for that person as you work. Stitch a favorite verse onto some fabric and pray it over yourself and your loved ones while you labor with thread and needle. The possibilities go hand in hand with our interests and hobbies.

Following on my friend's idea of our quiet time being like a date with God, how about adding details to make it more memorable and inspiring? When my kids were at home, they loved it when I got out the special china, used festive napkins, a beautiful table cloth, or some flowers for our family dinners. Once in a while, we'd cook something extra delicious, or get out the wine glasses for a festive drink, not because company was coming, but because it was just us at home together, and that was reason enough to celebrate. In the same way, spending time with God is something to celebrate!

What if we add a touch of celebration to our quiet times by lighting a candle, drinking a delicious tea or coffee in a beautiful cup, or bringing along something lovely, like a flower? Inspiring background music can add beauty and peace to our time with God. A pretty new journal, special pens, or artist paper and pencils can inspire us.

What if we add a touch of celebration to spending time with God?

TAKE A PERSONAL MINI-RETREAT

Does the word "retreat" conjure up thoughts like "Who has the time? Where could I go and how much would it cost?" What about thinking in terms of a mini-retreat? Of course, it would be lovely to go off somewhere to spend the weekend alone in a bed and breakfast, but you can also carve out a few hours for yourself in your own backyard while someone watches the kids. Grab a pocket Bible or a small backpack with a few supplies and take your quiet time outside. Sit on a park bench for a few minutes to read

Scripture and then take a prayer walk. Going on a bike ride somewhere nearby with a packed lunch could be the breath of fresh air your soul needs.

A personal retreat to spend focused time on your relationship with Jesus is a wonderful way to bring renewal to a spirit that's fallen into the doldrums. Use your retreat time for a spiritual activity you enjoy but never find time for. Read a Christian book, or experiment with art pencils and your journal. Read through a favorite book of the Bible or spend extended time in prayer. Pray through the acronym ACTS (Adoration, Confession, Thanksgiving, and Supplication) and use art paper to make a free-form drawing, chart, or collage, adding to it during each stage of your prayer time. Your artwork will serve as a memento you can come back to later to remember your conversation with God and continue praying.

Make friends with local parks in your area. The summer after I graduated from college and wasn't sure what I was going to do with my life, I made weekly trips to a botanical garden downtown and spent quiet time in the Japanese garden. As I listened to running water and looked at waterlilies and goldfish week after week, I could sense God speaking assurance into the confusion I felt, and my sense of trust deepened. Life has changed now, and I definitely can't make time for weekly excursions downtown, but a small park near my house has picnic tables. So once every month or two, whenever I can, I take my Bible and notebook to the park to sit under the trees, and I still hear that same quiet voice.

For those blessed to live near a beach or lake, a walk by the water might be the opportunity you need to remember God's love is deeper and wider than oceans. Let's not forget this word from Habakkuk 2:14: "For the earth will be filled with the knowledge of the glory of the Lord as the waters cover the sea."

Let's think outside the box when it comes to destinations and activities for a personal retreat. A quiet walk through a local museum might refresh and inspire our souls, especially when we follow it up with time for reading and journaling. We can take a prayer walk downtown and treat ourselves to sitting at an actual table in a coffee shop rather than grabbing a coffee to go.

When you have littles or school-aged kids, getting away by yourself can be downright impossible. If your husband is willing, maybe you can take advantage of family excursions to the beach or mountains to take a few minutes of personal time: a quick walk along the water or up a trail while he stays with the kids a few minutes. Let's remember the life-giving power of small steps here. Actually taking 15 minutes for ourselves today will do our soul more good than dreaming of the perfect 3-hour retreat that never happens.

Taking 15 minutes for ourselves today does our soul more good than the perfect 3-hour retreat that never happens.

HAVE FUN MAPPING OUT YOUR GOALS (IF IT'S YOUR CUP OF TEA)

For a change of pace if you enjoy it, leave aside regular Bible reading to spend a few days brainstorming and praying over your life vision and goals during your quiet time. What better time to set goals than when we're already spending time in God's presence and hopefully being led by Him? A couple of times a year, I take a few days to pray over the roles God has given me and determine a few goals for each one. I make what I call a vision map. Here are the steps to do it:

- Ask God for a life verse to give you direction the next three to six months.
- Consider the different roles you have: child of God, wife, mom, employee, home business entrepreneur, Bible study or ministry leader, whatever yours are. Pray over them. If you like, ask God to direct you to a Scripture verse for each role.
- Pray and ask God for guidance as you brainstorm for ideas of things you'd like to accomplish in each area of your life. Make a multi-colored mind map, using a different color for each life area or role and your ideas related to it.
- Once you have all your ideas down, prayerfully consider which ones God might be prompting you to turn into a few goals for the months ahead.
- Make a graphic organizer with your goals in different colors. Use washi tape or whatever

scrapbooking materials you like to make it pretty and put it somewhere you'll see it each day.

Friend, if your quiet time has fallen into the realm of Dullsville, you are not alone. It happens to all of us. Let's pray for renewal and ask God for grace to use more creativity in the time we spend with Him. Take a moment to consider what things you enjoy in life that you could bring into your quiet time. What small change could you make this week to freshen up your quiet time? What if you set aside 20 or 30 minutes this week to try a new creative pursuit?

> *What small change could you make this week to freshen up your quiet time?*

How about praying for God to transform our time with Him into a delight? Let's ask Him to give us hearts that delight in His Word and enjoy responding in prayer. Let's pray that He'll give us practical, creative wisdom to make quiet time more enjoyable. God is in the business of reviving hearts, so let's knock on His doors to ask for renewed enjoyment in the time we spend with Him. Since prayer is key to spiritual refreshment, let's talk about that next.

9

Help for Distracted, Side-Tracked Prayer Warriors

Distraction does me in when it comes to prayer. Approximately 45 seconds after I start praying, my mind starts to wander. Just like it did in Mrs. White's third grade math class. While Mrs. White explained the multiplication tables, I read books under my desk. During math class each day I'd travel in my mind across the United States in a covered wagon with Laura Ingalls Wilder to her *Little House on the Prairie.* Or I'd take a trip with E.B. White to the farm where Wilbur lived with Charlotte the spider in *Charlotte's Web.*

The only problem was each time I returned from my trips, Mrs. White would still be there. She'd ask me to recite the multiples of 4, and I'd stare at her blankly. When it came time for the cumulative multiplication test at the end of the semester, I failed miserably. I didn't learn the multiplication tables until my dad saw the "D" on my report card and sat with me every night for a week with homemade flashcards.

Distraction did me in when it came to math, and it's no different when it comes to prayer. I start to pray, but before I know it, I'm thinking about my grocery list, my latest project, or our Maltese poodle's urgent need to go to the vet for a trim. If you experience the same thing, I invite you to join me as we take a look at some of the obstacles that distract or discourage our prayer lives and what we can do about them.

GETTING PAST THE PRESSURE TO GET IT RIGHT

Prayer is one area of the Christian life where somehow I feel a pressure to get it right. After all, you have to be a strong prayer warrior to be an effective Christian, right? We all know we're supposed to put on the spiritual armor of God each day, enter boldly into God's throne room to receive mercy and grace, and pray with faith that moves mountains. Yes, these are truths from God's Word, but can I let you in on a secret? Sometimes I'm just plain old airheaded and absent-minded when I pray.

I love Max Lucado for reminding us we don't have to be prayer warriors with these words: "I'm a recovering prayer wimp. I doze off when I pray. My thoughts zig, then zag, then zig again. Distractions swarm like gnats on a summer night. If attention deficit disorder applies to prayer, I am affected."[1] His words free me to remember I don't have to aim for perfection when it comes to prayer. After all, striving for perfect is a sure recipe for crash and burn because if perfect praying is my goal, I'm defeated before I ever utter a word to God. Then after I start praying, distraction sets in, followed by self-doubt. *What kind of Christian am I, anyway? After all, surely a mature believer wouldn't have such problems with prayer.* Do you have similar thoughts? Let's move past self-judgment and the pressure to get it right.

Maybe we make it too hard to be a prayer warrior. Instead of awesome faith victories and one-hour prayer vigils, let's aim for small steps in the right direction. I'd rather be a prayer wimp who actually lifts up a few brief, heart-felt prayers to God in the morning and throughout the day than a wannabe prayer warrior who never gets around to doing the mountain-moving prayer she dreams of. Maybe God is more pleased that we can even imagine with the small prayer we lift up for our daughter's test or our son's broken leg. Perhaps the desperate prayer for patience during a traffic jam thrills His heart more than we know.

MOVING PAST DISCOURAGEMENT

If we're honest, distraction and the pressure to get it right aren't the only things that defeat us. Discouragement when answers don't come can also be a deterrent that keeps us from praying. It helps me to remember that prayer is more than standing in line at a fast food restaurant where I reel off a list of things I want from God and wait for Him to fill my order. Prayer is an amazing invitation to enter into relationship with the God who created the universe. Through prayer, we have the blessing of recognizing and enjoying His presence with us. We possess the privilege of offering worship, giving thanks, and presenting our requests to God. We have the opportunity to pour out our deepest feelings and learn to hear His quiet yet powerful voice speaking back to us.

Through prayer, we have the blessing of recognizing and enjoying God's presence with us.

Scripture tells us, "Ask and it will be given to you; seek and you will find; knock and the door will be opened to you" (Matthew 7:7). Yet we've all experienced the discouragement of not receiving the answer we hope for at the time we expect it.

For several years I've prayed for God to bring a young woman I love like a daughter back to Himself. For the first time ever, I feel like I understand what the father in the Parable of the Lost Boy must have felt like. My heart wrenches time after time while I watch my beloved prodigal daughter make choices I fear will take her further away from the God who longs to be her Heavenly Father. What pains me most is my own doubt over why the All-Powerful God doesn't deliver her from darkness or reveal Himself to her in a way she cannot deny, but at the same time I recognize that God may be working in ways I cannot see.

Perhaps you have a prodigal you love or a prayer request you dearly hope for. In situations like these, I like to remember Zechariah and Elizabeth. The first chapter of Luke tells us they were childless because Elizabeth was unable to conceive. How many times they must have asked God for a baby! What heartache they must have known as the years went by, and God didn't give them one. They had no way of knowing God was waiting for the perfect time in history to give them a child. They had no idea their son, John the Baptist, would announce the coming of the Messiah. God had far greater purposes than they could even imagine.

In God's perfect timing, the angel came with a message of hope: "Do not be afraid, Zechariah; your prayer has been heard. Your wife Elizabeth will bear you a son, and you are to call him John" (Luke 1:13). Two thousand years later, these words still speak encouragement to my heart: "Your prayer has been heard." They help me hold on to hope when my prayers seem to go unanswered, and they remind me God does hear our prayers. Just because we don't see an answer now doesn't mean one will never come. God listens and responds to His children's cries, but sometimes His plans go far beyond our small prayers.

Sometimes God's plans go far beyond our small prayers.

If you're going through discouragement in your prayer life, why not ask God to spark renewal? Ask Him to renew your vision for prayer and give you a fresh awareness of His presence with you during your quiet time and throughout your day.

This may sound crazy, but when I struggle with doubt in my prayer life, I ask God to encourage me by showing me one small answer. I pray He'll have mercy on my unbelief and give me one small sign that He hears me. And you know what? He answers this prayer of mine time and time again. One weekend while my dear "adopted" daughter stayed in our home, I told God I desperately needed some small sign He was at work in her life. Three hours later she shocked me by getting up to go to church with us, even though she'd said she wouldn't the night before. I remembered my small prayer that morning, and I recognized God's answer.

Maybe the best way past discouragement is to keep praying. Let's look now at some practical ways to move past distraction.

KEEP IT SIMPLE

The maxim "Pray as you can, not as you can't" frees me to keep it simple.[2] Sometimes we think we have to pray long and complicated prayers for God to hear us. For me, that's when distraction sets in most. I forget what it was I was praying for. When I lift up simple prayers, trusting that God hears me, I stay focused. God isn't waiting for us to hit upon the right wording before He answers us. He's not holding us to a minimum word count for prayer to work. He's delighted with the small steps we take to lift up our concerns.

> God isn't waiting for us to hit upon the right wording to answer our prayer.

Quiet time prayer can be as simple as moving through your to-do list or day planner and asking God to guide and bless each activity. It can be praying over a list of loved ones, lifting up each name and asking God to work in each life with a few simple sentences that express your heart for those you love. Whether I pray through the same list for a few days, or jot down a few new requests each morning, something about a list helps me keep prayer focused and simple.

PRAY OUT LOUD

Today I saw a "free soul" at the park, and it made me feel good. He was marching along our neighborhood walking trail belting out a loud song, which let everyone know how thoroughly he enjoyed the sounds coming out of his earbuds. It made me smile because lately I pray out loud as I walk my dog. Not as brave as Mr. Free Spirit, I wait until no one else is close to me on the trail, and I murmur out words. When other people approach me, I kind of hope they'll think I'm talking to my dog. Then I shift to a few minutes of silent prayer until I'm alone again. Hopefully the other walkers and runners don't even notice my quiet mumblings, but maybe they hear me and think I'm a bona fide basket case. Either way, I'm glad for a few minutes of focused prayer, and I'm pretty sure I don't attract as much attention as the free spirit guy.

Praying aloud helps me stay focused, and it reminds me prayer is a daily conversation with God. I can talk to Him just as I talk to my husband or my kids; talking out loud helps me remember He actually hears me and anchors my thoughts to our conversation.

PRAY GOD'S WORD

Scripture acts like a springboard for prayer. We read God's Words, and prayer is our chance to respond. The words of Scripture provide a powerful focus to a wandering mind, and praying God's Word back to Him has several benefits:

- **Direction:** God's Word guides and directs us when we don't know what to ask Him for. As we pray the words of Scripture, we know we're praying in line with God's will. When life gets hard and heartache leaves us speechless, it gives us the words we need.
- **Power:** Let's not forget the Bible is a living book. As we read and pray it, the Holy Spirit brings it to life. When we declare the truth of God's Word, we unleash His power in our lives.
- **Focus:** If our minds wander, we can always go back to the scripture that sparked our prayer. When our faith flounders, the Bible is a steadfast anchor; it gives us words to declare and truth to stand on.

When we declare the truth of God's Word, we unleash His power in our lives.

Something beautiful happens in our Spirits when we let God's Word lead and inform our prayers. Here are two ways to do it:

Let God's Word Shape Your Prayer

After you read a passage during your quiet time, respond in prayer. Did you see any blessings to thank God for? Did you read anything that moved your heart to praise Him? Sometimes when we read Scripture, God shows us a sinful attitude we need to confess or something we did that we need to ask forgiveness for.

When we pray God's words back to Him, we know we're praying His will for ourselves and those we love. Let what you read spark prayer for your own growth. What qualities and character traits do you see that you want? What commands do you need to obey? Pray those things for yourself. Let God's Word show you how to pray for your husband, children, and friends as well.

Pray the prayers of the Bible

Scripture records the heart cry of men and women who loved and followed God. In Genesis, we can read Abraham's conversations with the Creator, and we have the privilege of reading Moses' prayers of blessing for the tribes of Israel (Deuteronomy 33). The Psalms let us in on the praises, petitions, laments, and even rants that David lifted up to His Lord. The Gospels show us how Jesus prayed to His Father. We read Paul's petitions and prayers in his letters to the churches. As we read those words, they teach us how to relate to God.

Especially for those times when I feel like I'm at the end of my prayer rope, and I don't have words or concentration or faith to believe God even hears me, somehow it bolsters my faith to pray along with passages like these:

- 1 Chronicles 29:10-13 (David's prayer of praise and thanks near the end of his life)
- 1 Samuel 2:1-10 (Hannah's prayer)
- Psalm 51 (David's confession of sin and prayer for a pure heart)
- Luke 1:46-55 (Mary's worship song)
- Matthew 6:9-13 (The Lord's Prayer)
- Ephesians 1:15-23, Ephesians 3:14-21, Colossians 1:9-12 (Paul's prayers)

PRAYER JOURNALING

I'm not a fan of scrolling through Pinterest or Instagram to look at the beautiful, artistic Bible journaling I see there. Instead of feeling inspired, I feel like throwing in the towel. Because there's no way my journaling will ever look like theirs.

But that's okay.

Prayer journaling is still the best way I know to combat distraction as I pray, so I'm going to keep at it, even if my journal pages look awkward, off-center, and have scribbles where I misspelled words or wrote the wrong word altogether because my mind went AWOL. Even if my prayer lists and maps look less than perfect, journaling helps me stay focused. Here are some ideas for you to try, but only when and if they inspire you. Because the last thing you need is one more obligation. Prayer journaling doesn't make anyone more spiritual or mature; it is a tool to help us find focus.

> *Prayer journaling doesn't make anyone more spiritual; it is only a tool to help us focus.*

Drawing out Your Prayers

Mind you, I use the word "drawing" loosely here because what I do is actually doodling or scribbling in different colors while I pray. My hand moving over the page keeps my mind engaged. Sometimes I end up with a design that's pleasing to the eye, and some days it's a messy hodgepodge full of scribbling. Yet both the pretty design and the messy hodgepodge help me pray.

I learned how to incorporate drawing and scribbling into my prayer life from Sybil MacBeth and her creative, refreshing book, *Praying in Color: Drawing a New Path to God.*[3] Sybil recommends starting simply: draw a shape and then write a name inside. As you pray for that person, color in the shape or make a design around it.

When you're finished, draw another shape next to it and write in another name. You can use this same basic technique whether you're praying for people you love, events to come, or qualities you want in your life.

Adding in a few names or topics each morning, I typically take a couple of days to make a drawing I'll use like a prayer list for several weeks or even months. Sometimes I write a few words inside or around the shape with a person's name; these words remind me of my prayer requests. Usually I choose a different color for each person or topic, so I have a colorful list or drawing. Getting it out to look at during my quiet time reminds me of what I hope God will do in the people I love.

Prayer Mapping

Do you ever feel like your prayer life consists of asking God for things you need just to make it through the day? For me, sometimes praying can feel like giving my order at McDonalds. I give God a list of what I need today or this week, but this narrows my vision. Basically I'm praying for French fries and extra ketchup, forgetting all about the amazing banquet of blessings God wants to give me. I lose sight of my greater purpose in life, my vision for serving God, and all the spiritual blessings available to me in Christ.

What helps get me out of this rut is making a prayer map, a visual representation of the bigger picture of my spiritual life and what I really want from God. It keeps me on track praying for things that truly matter and helps me to not lose sight of the path ahead of me. A prayer map encourages me to see long term goals, not just the short term needs to make it through today.

Here's how to make a prayer map:

1. Ask God to guide you as you think and brainstorm over 6-8 big picture goals or prayer requests. Currently mine are greater faith, healing, joy, anointing, provision, a life that honors God, and passion for Christ in my kids' hearts. You might want renewal in your marriage or more fruit of the Spirit in your life. Maybe you have a work-related goal you want to pray for, such as a new job by the end of the year or a new business venture. Ask God to guide you and then trust that He's speaking as thoughts come to mind.

2. On a sheet of paper, or a double-page spread in your journal, write down your prayer requests in the form of words or phrases, using a different color for each one. Space them out, so that you have room around each word. Draw a circle around each one, and outside it, jot down a few thoughts, one-sentence prayers, or related requests in the same color. If one comes to mind, write out an encouraging Bible verse that speaks to you on this topic. Use your personal brand of creativity; there's no right or wrong way to do it.

About once a year, I take a week or so to make a new prayer map, and I keep a tab marker on that page in my journal, so I can refer back to it later and pray. Usually I end up memorizing it, so I don't really have to look, but I still do. Because something about looking at that map, with requests written out in different colors, keeps my mind focused on prayer. I also pray through some of those "big picture" requests while I walk my dog in the park each morning.

These suggestions are for helping us to focus and make prayer more meaningful during our quiet times, but Jesus is with us all day long. Even after we close our Bibles or finish our daily prayer time, His Holy Spirit remains with us. His power, peace, love, and hope are always available; we just have to ask for them.

God's power, peace, love and hope are always available when we ask for them.

We don't have to be prayer warriors or prayer experts. Even absent-minded prayer wimps can turn their hearts towards Jesus, one faltering prayer at a time, and receive more of His abundant resources throughout the day. Let's look next at ideas for keeping company with our Savior during our busy days.

10

After Your Quiet Time: Taking Jesus with You into Your Day

Wouldn't it be great if all we had to do in life was drink endless cups of tea or coffee, read devotionals, spend time journaling, listen to worship music, and do creative Bible study? Sure, we might get bored after a while, but we'd live with less stress. I think that's why I always secretly wished to be a nun.

However, even the most inspiring quiet time must come to an end. We've got kids to dress, work projects to turn in, errands to run, and meals to make. In fact, a meaningful quiet time is not an end-all to our spiritual lives; instead it's a springboard for inviting more of God into the rest of our day. It's a training ground; learning to relate to God during a few minutes of stillness helps us interact with Him later while we're on the go. After all, even most nuns work! In reality, I suspect they do than my day-dreaming girlhood self could imagine. Life is so much more than a spiritual retreat. One of the ways we reflect God's image is by engaging in creative, productive labor. Yet at the same time, He created us for fellowship with Himself.

A meaningful quiet time is a springboard for inviting more of God into the rest of our day.

Consider this verse: "God is faithful, who has called you into fellowship with his Son, Jesus Christ our Lord" (1 Corinthians 1:9). I love this reminder that although God calls me to many roles and tasks, He also desires that I enjoy companionship with His Son. I don't think we're called into fellowship with Jesus for just a few minutes each morning, do you? Our Lord doesn't expect us to end our devotional time by saying, "I'll check back in tomorrow morning at 6:30." Instead, God intends for us to keep company with His Son throughout each day.

CAN WE REALLY TAKE JESUS WITH US?

The thought of taking Jesus with me wherever I go both motivates and puzzles me. I mean, He's God, so it's not like I can just stick Him in my pocket, right? I wish it were that easy. But just like we can invite a friend to come along with us, so can we invite Jesus to join us wherever we go.

In fact, we actually do carry Jesus around inside us. Take a look at these two verses:

"I pray that out of his glorious riches he may strengthen you with power through his Spirit in your inner being, so that Christ may dwell in your hearts through faith..." Ephesians 3:16-17a

"To them God has chosen to make known among the Gentiles the glorious riches of this mystery, which is Christ in you, the hope of glory." Colossians 1:27

By some amazing mystery we cannot fully comprehend, the Spirit of God came to live inside us when we put our faith in Christ. Jesus lives in us. Our hearts become His home. He goes with us, but we need to remind ourselves of this often during our day. That's why I like the image of taking Him with me.

Last year, two friends from out of town came to visit me in the summertime. I realized they had no agenda other than to spend time with me and my family and bless us. They brought gifts and let me know they didn't want me to go to any trouble to entertain them. At some point in the day, I needed to run a few errands, but it was so hot outside that I didn't want to inconvenience them.

"I have to go out for an hour," I said. "But feel free to stay home. You'd get fried outside."

"Oh, can we come too? We'd be happy to go along," they answered. "We just want to spend time with you." So they came along that day, and I realized how refreshing it was just to have someone alongside me. Later that afternoon, we had snacks together, and they asked how they could pray for me. They took our family out to dinner and left the next morning. I realized that just maybe I'd seen Jesus with skin on. Surely He wants to be that kind of friend, the kind that comes alongside.

DOING EVERYTHING FOR HIM

One of my closest friends is a gifted teacher, mentor, and Bible study leader. I keep telling her she should go into full-time ministry, but she tells me she already *is* in full-time ministry working as a university instructor. She has a burning vision to serve and glorify God through her secular profession, and she probably has a higher, broader view of what it means to serve Him than I do.

Her view of serving God through serving students is right in line with Colossians 3:23-24: "Whatever you do, work at it with all your heart, as working for the Lord, not for human masters, since you know that you will receive an inheritance from the Lord as a reward. It is the Lord Christ you are serving."

God is looking for people who want to live for Him as they work in kitchens, offices, classrooms, movie theaters, and supermarkets. Whether you're cooking the 5,237th meal or preparing a Bible study for Wednesday night, your work brings God glory when you do it for Him and through Him, relying on His strength.

> *Your work brings God glory when you do it for Him and through Him, relying on His strength.*

What if we go through our days, lifting up each task to Him? What if we stop before each new assignment to recognize God and ask Him for help? We can lift brief prayers like these: "Father, I need your help now. I want to do this for you. Would you give me the strength and wisdom I need?" And what if we finish each task by giving simple thanks for the grace He gives? We'll have plenty to talk about with Jesus all day long, and no telling how much more effective we'll become for the sake of His Kingdom and glory.

TURNING TO HIM IN TRIAL: OUR FIRST RESPONSE?

Healthcare and public service organizations say the actions taken in the first moments of an emergency are critical and can save lives. If a person collapses, bystanders should first check for breathing. In an earthquake, people should drop, take cover, and hold on. Part of emergency training involves repeating the necessary first steps until they become automatic.

What is our first response in our troubling moments? I want mine to be Jesus.

During the first years of our marriage, my husband travelled up to 25% of the time. Although he rarely travels anymore, I still joke about how José's getting on a plane is a sure recipe for disaster and emergencies at home. I remember one particularly memorable trip he took during a year our family lived stateside. I drove him to the airport, and the very minute he walked through the sliding glass doors to the terminal, the car window slid down into the door by itself in a permanently open position. No amount of pushing the electric button would close it. *Awesome.*

I went home to make an appointment at the auto shop and taped a plastic garbage bag to the window frame as a temporary solution. *Classy, I know.* The next day, the toilet clogged up in our family bathroom, and I fell apart. After 15 minutes of searching the house for a plunger, I stormed out to the car to make the 15-minute drive to Target. "Why can't we be like regular people who already have a plunger at home," I fumed. "Why do these things always happen when José is gone? And why can't I get this blasted window shut!" It was 100 degrees inside the car, and for the first five minutes, I stewed behind the steering wheel as I drove. Then it occurred to me to turn some worship music on.

As I listened to the strains of praise, my heart changed. My mood lightened. An open car window and clogged toilet were not the end of the world. God was going to get me through the glitches. I started praying for joy and a new attitude.

When I got back home, I still couldn't unclog that toilet. In fact, things got worse. Don't ask me how, but somehow the bathroom door shut and locked itself on the inside. I gave up and decided to call the plumber, yet my attitude had changed, and I knew God had His reasons for allowing my mini-emergency. Maybe He wanted to teach me joy and patience?

I couldn't help but laugh as I made the phone call. "You're not going to believe this," I said. "Our toilet is clogged, but the bathroom door is locked from the inside, and we can't get it open." You'd better believe I was more than happy to write out a 95 dollar check to that plumber three hours later.

You and I both know we encounter trials a lot more challenging than clogged toilets behind locked doors.

We've made emergency room runs and sat through funeral parlor wakes. Whether we encounter small, daily difficulties, or life-altering crises, let's make turning to Jesus our first response. He holds all the grace we need to get through whatever we're facing. As we practice turning to Him for grace in the small things, we're building habits we need to make Him our first response when life throws us the hard curveballs that threaten to knock us down.

Let's make turning to Jesus our first response in troubling moments.

In long grocery store lines and traffic jams, let's lift our eyes to the One who can renew our joy even when daily life threatens to squeeze it out of us. Whether we're meeting with an irate boss or our child's teacher, let's turn our hearts to the source of all wisdom, so we'll know how to respond in difficult situations. God gives grace that goes beyond our understanding, so let's go back to Him often during our day. We'll receive what we need when we turn to Him.

TAKE GOD'S WORD WITH YOU

For me, one of the best ways to take Jesus into my day is to take His words with me. Scripture is a never-ending source of strength and hope. I want to internalize what I read so that it becomes part of me, a guide for my thoughts and feelings.

Colossians 3:16 says, "Let the word of Christ dwell in you richly, teaching and admonishing one another in all wisdom, singing psalms and hymns and spiritual songs, with thankfulness in your hearts to God" (ESV). These words remind me that with God's Word inside me, I'll always have words of hope and wisdom for others, as well as a song of grace for my own heart as I go about my day.

I have a long way to go, but I'm taking baby steps. Here are some things you can try along with me.

Let it Change Your Day

When you read a passage during your quiet time, ask yourself, "How can this make a difference in my day?" Maybe you see a character quality you want to develop. Perhaps you see an attitude to embrace or a way to serve others. Jot down an application point or a one-sentence prayer. The "Word for Today" idea I described earlier helps me have something concrete I can easily remember later. As you go about your day, come back to that thought, word, or brief prayer. Let it temper your reactions to people and circumstances. Come back to it at lunchtime to ask yourself, "How am I practicing this today?" Then remember it again before bedtime.

Memorize It

As I mentioned before, I have a little green book where I've written different Bible verses I've memorized. Although

I'm not as consistent as I'd like with memorizing Scripture, I treasure my green book. It literally helps me to take God's Word with me. Sometimes I keep it in my purse so I can get it out in line at the grocery store, on the metro, at the doctor's office, or while waiting for a friend.

Use Notecards

I have a friend who types out Bible verses on a notetaking app for her phone, but I'm a pen and paper girl. I like to physically write out a verse on a notecard and actually tape it up near my desk, or carry it in my pocket so I can get it out to look at.

Somedays I forget all about taking God's words with me. I carry my Scripture memory book around for days without cracking it open, or I write a verse on a notecard and lose it. I pen a one-sentence prayer and forget all about it. But other days I go back to it, and God's Word works in me. I'm not getting it perfect, but I'm slowly making progress. Simple steps forward, taken over time, add up to growth in God.

> *Simple steps taken over time add up to growth in God.*

PRAYER ON THE GO

A natural way to remember Jesus goes with us throughout the day is to keep an ongoing conversation with Him, just like we do with anyone else we spend lots of time with.

He's in the car with us while we wait in the school drop-off line. He's there at our desk, and He attends every meeting at work. Come evening, He hangs out in the kitchen while we cook dinner or unpack our takeout bags.

Why don't we talk to Jesus more? Maybe it's because we think of prayer as a list of praises or petitions, and somehow we need to be in the right frame of mind for that. We imagine we must have our thoughts tidily collected and ready to present to the Lord. But really, prayer is an ongoing conversation and relationship with God.

Prayer Prompts

My friend Kathryn Shirey first taught me about prayer prompts. She chooses something ordinary about her day that will serve as a trigger to remind her to pray. For example, Kathryn prays thanksgiving prayers in her car when she stops at red lights.[1] Inspired by her idea, I started praying for family members each morning while I walk down three flights of stairs to get to the ground floor of our building.

A few years ago, the idea of prayer prompts helped me reconnect with gratitude during a trying time. As I mentioned before, my family and I lived overseas for sixteen years, but when my son started college, we relocated to Dallas, Texas, for nine months. I had a close relationship with my son, so empty nest syndrome hit me hard. At the same time, all of us, especially my daughter, were dealing with the culture shock that happens when one returns home after years of living overseas. Added to the mix was a car that constantly broke down.

Tears overflowed many days, but no matter how the day had gone, one thing helped shift my perspective. Each evening as I made the rounds about the house to close the wooden shutters in the windows, I'd thank God for the blessings of the day. In the morning, as I opened them to let light in, I'd thank Him for a new gift of twenty-four hours. That simple practice helped me gain a more positive outlook.

Prayer List on the Go

For years, I've been making little prayer booklets to carry around with me. I fold a piece of typing paper long-ways down the center and then make an accordion fold, so it will stand up sideways in the shape of an "M." This gives me four faces on each side. On the cover I write a Bible verse that speaks to my current life season, so I can turn it into a daily prayer. To make a prayer list, I use one face for each day of the week and write a list of names or things I want to pray for that day. If you want to see what mine looks like, I shared it on my blog in a post called "One Simple Way to Pray on the Go."[2] I make a new prayer booklet several times a year; the one I'm currently using looks more like a prayer map than a list. I've covered its pages with colorful prayer drawings, including names of loved ones, big picture prayer requests, and the fruit of the spirit I want in my own life.

I carry my prayer booklet around in my purse and set it on the dashboard of my car or on the kitchen counter while I'm cooking or cleaning up. Being the distracted woman I am, many days I misplace it, but after several weeks of using it, I can more or less remember the content anyway. However, when I find it again, I always set it back out where I can see it. Seeing that booklet serves like a prayer trigger for me; I tend to pray more when I see it.

One-Sentence or One-Word Prayers

One of my favorite ways to pray simply is to lift up that one-sentence prayer I write many mornings in response to one verse or word I choose from my daily Bible reading. Sometimes remembering my one word sparks a spontaneous prayer, or I just lift up that word itself as a prayer. Having a single sentence or word in mind saves me on harried, stressful days when I can't calm my mind enough to think of much else. It centers my thoughts and my heart back on Jesus.

A One-Day Experiment to Try

What if we spent a whole day focused on having an ongoing conversation with Jesus? What if we made it a point to talk to Him about our daily activities, no matter how mundane? I'm trying to experiment with ongoing, comfortable prayer while I write this book, and it helps me remember Jesus is near me. We don't have to pray fancy prayers. Simple words like these please our Savior:

- Thank you for blessings like this delicious coffee.
- Will you help me with this?
- Help me show love to this person.
- Thank you for this fun time with my kids.
- Will you guide me right now?

Our dearest, most faithful Friend never leaves our side, and He longs for us to acknowledge His presence by speaking to Him. Jesus loves for us to honor Him by doing our work for Him and relying on His strength instead of our own. So let's keep company with our Savior. Surely our work load will seem lighter with His help, and our burdens will lift as we give our worries to Him one by one. Even on our most difficult days, the constant presence of Jesus brings strength, hope, and light.

> Even on our most difficult days,
> the constant presence of Jesus
> brings strength, hope, and light.

11

How to Keep Going When Life Gets Hard?

"Mrs. Cruz, I need you to call Dr. Smelter's office right away. It's urgent," said the voice on the recording. "We need to discuss your blood test results." I'd stepped out of a meeting to listen to the message, and I replayed it several times to see if I was hearing right. Did her voice really sound as tense as I thought?

Why would the nurse leave a message like that? Didn't she know not to freak out the doctor's patients? Was she having a bad day or was she just whacked out by stress? After a few hours of phone tag, I learned the iron level in my blood was at 6.8, much lower than the normal range of 12-15 for women.

"I don't understand how you're walking around," she said. "If you feel faint at all, please go to the emergency room immediately! We're going to have to do some testing to get to the bottom of this." She said she'd schedule me right away for appointments with a gastroenterologist to check for internal bleeding and a hematologist for cancer screening.

I hung up wondering why she was exaggerating, until I did a Google search on severe anemia. Along with internal bleeding, the list of possible causes included cancer, kidney disease, and bone marrow disorders; apparently, I was also at risk for a heart attack. I forced myself to shut my laptop and hoped my kids wouldn't run the same search.

I had to admit I'd been feeling exhausted and headachy for months, but I refused to worry about it. In fact, the gastroenterologist I saw said the results must be a mistake because I looked too healthy.

"How could you be walking around looking healthy with such low hemoglobin levels?" he said. He ordered another test, but his phone call two days later rocked my world in the worst of ways.

"Mrs. Cruz, your hemoglobin level has dropped to 6. You need to go to the emergency room for a blood transfusion today. I'm concerned you could go into heart failure."

Thoughts racing, I did another Google search, called my husband and our insurance company, and began to pack a few things to take to the hospital. A few hours later, I shivered in a blue and white cotton gown. I tried not to look at the bag of blood hanging overhead and the thin red tube and needle attached to my arm. I thought about how I could hide this from my mother because I didn't want her to be scared like I was.

During that first hospital visit, I had no idea I'd go through six weeks of having my arms poked and my body prodded and scanned, all the while wondering if I really could have cancer. I didn't know that cappuccino flavoring wouldn't disguise the taste of a liter of barium sulfate one bit, and I certainly didn't know daily visits to the hospital or doctor could leave you waking up with the goal of making it through till bedtime.

One simple index card got me through.

Of course, God was the One who helped me through it, but on the days when my mind couldn't think straight enough to get anything from Scripture, I carried around a simple index card with a verse I'd chosen for myself:

"Do not fear, for I am with you; do not be dismayed, for I am your God. I will strengthen you and help you; I will uphold you with my righteous right hand."
Isaiah 41:10

That card was the first thing I looked at on my bedside table when I woke up in the morning. I'd put it on the kitchen counter and the car dashboard. Each time I read it, I'd hear God's voice saying, "Don't be afraid. I'll strengthen you and help you." That simple promise gave me a sense of peace and relief. As I repeated my verse to myself, to God, and to whoever would listen, my confidence in God's care for me grew. I didn't know what would happen, but I knew God was with me, and He'd hold me up no matter what.

WHEN YOU WONDER IF GOD'S THERE AND IF HE'S GOOD

You may be going through a hard spot right now, and if you're not, my life experience tells me you will be soon. Hardships and heartaches are part of this life, but God promises to be with us and hold us up. Sometimes all we can do is hang on to the truth that He'll never leave us. No matter what happens, we have the blessing and grace of God's presence. In all things, we have a Helper who never fails us.

For me, choosing one simple truth to hang on to was life-altering when my life was falling apart. I'd repeat it over and over to myself at the doctor's office before each blood test and medical procedure. I'd close my eyes, breathe in deep, and tell myself, "You are not alone. Your God is with you, so don't be discouraged." And I want to tell you the same thing today. No matter what is happening in your life right now, your God is with you, and He will hold you up with His powerful hand. Even if you feel like you're coming to the end of your rope, He will strengthen you for your next steps.

Another plain truth I hang on to in troubling times is this: "Give thanks to the Lord, for He is good, His love endures forever" (Psalm 118:29). The simple act of giving thanks is life-transforming when life gets tough. Even when you have to look hard, you can always find something to give thanks for, and remembering that one thing can lift your spirits.

Recalling God's goodness and love help shift our focus off ourselves and our problems and onto Him and His power. Rehearsing a simple truth in our minds transforms our thoughts and give us hope to hang on to.

Recalling God's goodness and love shifts our focus away from our problems and towards His power.

EMERGENCY CARE FOR OUR HEARTS AND MINDS

As it turned out, doctors didn't find anything seriously wrong with me. My hemoglobin levels began to rise when I took iron supplements. Words can't describe the light, airy feeling of relief when I walked out of my last appointment with good news. We celebrated for a few days, but life didn't get easier.

The following month, we moved back to the Middle East after nine months stateside, only to experience the uncertainty of living through a political coup attempt. On our television screens, we watched the government crush the military coup, declare a national state of emergency, and imprison thousands of people. We clearly felt God calling us to remain in the country and felt safe enough, yet I'd be lying if I said I never felt fear.

On top of that, in a few short months, medical bills started rolling in like an ocean tide. On the one hand, I still felt the joyous relief of having reasonably good health; on the other hand, it was hard to live worry-free under the stress of political unrest and tight finances. We wondered how we'd be able to continue paying for our son's college while our bank account shrunk with each medical bill. The month we had to pay to renew our residence permit, our refrigerator broke, and I've already mentioned how I wondered if we'd still have money to eat by the end of the month.

The government had declared a state of emergency, and I declared a state of emergency in my mind and heart. So I made myself what I called an emergency care kit. It was nine scriptures written out in different colors on a two-page spread of my journal, and I read those verses to myself every morning. They gave my mind something to wrap itself around when I felt like I just couldn't go on anymore. They helped me back then, and even now during times of trouble, I recopy my emergency kit, tweaking it by adding in a new verse or deleting an old one.

Reading through my emergency care verses helps me recalibrate my thoughts to the truth of God's Word. The first passage is the promise of Isaiah 26:3-4. "You keep him in perfect peace whose mind is stayed on you, because he trusts in you. Trust in the Lord forever, for the Lord God is an everlasting rock." These words help me make the decision to park my mind on God and His promises. He is the eternal Rock I can always trust.

Faith grows when we make the decision to park our minds on God and His promises.

What verses do you go back to time and time again when you need encouragement? Maybe you can take time to make yourself an emergency care kit, too. Rather than waiting until you have time to embark on a long project you have to do in one sitting, why not take a few minutes to write out one verse each day? You'll be done in a week or so. If you're going through a difficult season now, it might give you some hope to hang your heart on. If you're living through a happy time, you can still take advantage of an opportunity to prepare yourself better for the future.

WHEN THINGS DON'T WORK OUT LIKE WE HOPE

Things worked out for me after my medical scare, but maybe for you they haven't. Faith encourages us to hope for the best, but that best doesn't always come like we expect. We've all had times when life didn't work out as we hoped. I've experienced disappointments: when the man I thought God told me I'd marry broke off our engagement, or when I had to tell my kids that their grandmother back in El Salvador died while we were living overseas.

My friend Lisa Appelo knows the pain of heartache, grief, and loss better than I do. She went to bed one night with her 42-year-old husband Dan and woke early the next morning to his labored breathing. Quickly realizing it was a life-threatening emergency, she woke up her kids to call 911. While the ambulance travelled to her house, an operator talked her through administering CPR to her husband.

Lisa says she kept thinking, "Surely there is no way I am giving CPR to my high school sweetheart, the man I just kissed goodnight." After paramedics loaded her husband into an ambulance, she left the kids at home to go to the hospital. "I will never, ever forget seeing them huddled together on the floor of the boys' room, sobbing," she writes.[1]

Emergency room doctors and nurses worked for an hour to revive her husband before finally giving up. After 26 years of marriage, Dan died. Lisa was left alone, to walk through grief and take on the responsibility of raising seven kids.

Friends and family came around her as she walked the dark, lonely road of brokenness. Lisa found help and hope in the love of friends, books on grief, and worship songs, but nothing helped her more than going to God's Word each day. She called it "the daily exchange." She'd go to God with her grief, fears, and hopelessness, and exchange her thoughts for the truth in His Word. She describes it like this:

"Every single day, as I went to God in pain and brokenness and opened the Bible to see what He had for me that day, He set my feet on the Rock and anchored my soul in hope… Each morning I've come to my Bible time and exchanged my worry for God's peace. My despair for His hope. My pain for His promise. My feelings for God's truth."[2]

Seven years have passed since her husband died, but God walked Lisa through it. The grief of loss never completely fades, but God has restored joy: Lisa's oldest kids have gone to college now, gotten married, and she even has a grandbaby! God has given Lisa a heart to reach young widows like herself with hope and encouragement, and He is using her to impact others.

God carried Lisa through the hard times, and if you're battling grief, pain, or sickness today, friend, He will carry you through too. Stay as near to Him as you can.

GET REAL WITH GOD

Pain clouds our vision. It can lead us to think God isn't there and life is hopeless. When it seems God doesn't come through for us like we expect, we feel disappointment, and that disappointment can lead us to doubt. Is God really there? Is He good? Does He love us?

If you're in that hurting spot right now where it feels like life has left you reeling and you wonder if God really loves you or if He's even there, I want to encourage you to just get real with Him. You don't have to put on your happy, holy face to meet with God. Just show up with your pain, your disappointment and your loss. Bring it all. Bring all of you. Bring all of who you are and what you are feeling. Let Him have your doubts, fears, and questions.

> *You don't have to put on your happy, holy face to meet with God. You can also bring Him your pain and disappointment.*

Friend, keep showing up to spend time with God, even if it's just to sit in silence. Hold on to this promise: "Weeping may last through the night, but joy comes with the morning" (Psalm 30:5b NLT). During dark times, it helps me remember that joy will come sooner or later, and until it does, I will keep showing up. I will continue clinging to hope until God restores it fully in my heart.

When pain rubs my heart raw, and sadness or bitterness overwhelm me, I return to the simple. When life gets hard, I go into survival mode. I can't think about much, so I just focus on showing up and keeping it real, keeping it simple. Here are some ways to show up and hold on to God when life gets hard.

Bring Him all your Sorrows

Recently I experienced a deep healing time with God as I just poured out to Him a list of all my losses and grievances. Initially I just lifted each one to Him in prayer. Friends, it was not a holy moment. It was ranting and railing and pouring out my heart. It was tears shed as I grieved over a list of losses and disappointments that hurt. Later, I actually made a list in my journal, and I cannot describe the healing I felt. I do not know how God worked restoration in my heart as I did this, but He did. It was a miracle.

Sit in Silence

Sometimes our grief is so great that there are no words. All we can do is sit in silence. We need to be still and know He is God. If you're experiencing one of those wordless times, ask God to pour out over you a deep sense of His presence with you. Imagine yourself in God's lap and let Him hold you close. Remember His everlasting arms: "The eternal God is your refuge, and his everlasting arms are under you" (Deuteronomy 33:27, NLT).

Read a Psalm

When pain and problems, trial and trouble take up residence in my thought life, it's hard to think straight. I wish I could focus on a passage of Scripture, but there are moments in my life when I just can't do it. So I go back to Psalms. Since I read a Psalm daily during my good times anyway, they're familiar comfort and encouragement when I just can't handle Bible reading. Psalms run the gamut from down-and-out discouragement to roof-raising praise. The words meet my needs time and time again, offering simple, familiar reassurance through lines like this:

- "The Lord is my Shepherd, I lack nothing." (Psalm 23:1)
- "Whoever dwells in the shelter of the Most High will rest in the shadow of the Almighty." (Psalm 91:1)
- "Yes, my soul, find rest in God; my hope comes from Him." (Psalm 62:5)
- "You are my strength, I sing praise to you; you, God are my fortress, my God on whom I can rely." (Psalm 59:17)

- "You, LORD, keep my lamp burning; my God turns my darkness into light." (Psalm 18:28)

Remember and Receive God's Love

For me, returning to the simple things also means remembering God's great love. Scripture tells us love is the foundation of who God is and why He sent Jesus to die on the cross for us. On hard days, I ask God to show me His love all over again and I read scriptures about it. It does my soul good to sit still a moment, ask God to pour His love over me, and open my hands heavenward. As I whisper, "Lord, I receive your love," the Holy Spirit touches my heart every time.

Sing or Listen to a Song Each Day

My daughter says that music engages her heart like nothing else, and I have to agree. When our hearts are too battered and bruised for our minds to think straight, worship music brings healing. A few minutes spent in worship can help us gain a new perspective as we look upward towards God and remember His wisdom and power.

> When our hearts are too battered and bruised for our minds to think straight, worship brings healing.

KEEP SHOWING UP

One thing I've noticed about trials and hard times is that most of them eventually do end. Good times come again. I've had health scares, but today I'm alive and mostly well. My husband and I have gone through tight times with our finances, but we look back and see how God provided. In dark times, it helps to remember nothing lasts forever. Sooner or later, joy *does* come with the morning.

Sometimes the hard time doesn't end as we'd like, but God changes and enables us. My friend Lisa is still a widow, but God is using her to encourage many lives, and today she gives thanks for her beautiful family.

If we keep showing up to spend time with God each day during times of trial, we find more of Him. He helps us grow stronger, and He shows us purpose in our pain. His Word makes us wiser; it gives us a dose of healthy perspective when life looks overwhelming. Our struggles are not in vain because God is making something beautiful out of our lives.

12

The Reward of Showing up: More of God

We all have our desperate places where we urgently need more of God. As much as I love the phrase, "my happy place," and all the joyful, peaceful images it brings to mind, I have to admit I don't spend all my life there. I have desperate places too, where I seem to hang out a lot, if I'm honest. We all have our desperate places where we need more of God. We have those crazy woman moments when we could use more of God's peace and those lonely, depressed woman moments when we need more of His love. We go through times of plummeting hormones or chemical imbalances when we need more joy. Then there are all those times when we're not quite sure what we need, but we know we need more of it.

Yes, please. Lord, give me more of whatever it is I need.

A "desperate place" describes where I was when I burst into tears on the front porch of a family I didn't know in front of a perplexed man I'd never even seen before. He looked at me like he wondered if I had a few screws loose or just needed hormone therapy.

As I mentioned before, several years ago my family left our Middle East Home and relocated to Dallas, Texas, for nine months. Landing in a new city where I hardly knew a soul and sending my first born off to college took their toll. Never expecting to feel the empty nest syndrome so strongly, I felt sad and lonely for weeks. So I brightened up when I received an invitation to join a women's Bible study. I mustered up my courage to call the number, and a friendly woman answered.

"We'll be meeting on Wednesday nights," she said, "but I don't have the address yet. Can you call me back?"

However, the following Wednesday when I called for the address, I was disappointed.

"Oh, I am so sorry," she said. "I don't know what happened, but we forgot to call you. We decided to change the meeting to Tuesday nights, and we had our first meeting last night! I feel terrible! Can you join us next week?"

Even though this didn't help my loneliness one bit, I decided not to take it personally. I figured if this woman was anything like me, she had a lot on her plate, so I jotted down the address she gave me. The following Tuesday I rushed to make dinner for my family, so I could leave for Bible study. I may or may not have stressed out over what to wear, and I put on extra deodorant in case nerves overtook me during the harrowing drive to an unknown destination in a new city of 5,000,000 people. I took a brave gulp before heading out the driveway armed with my GPS and Google Maps.

Half an hour later, a bewildered man answered when I knocked on the door.

"Um. The Bible study isn't meeting here tonight. They changed the place." he said. "Let me call my wife."

He handed me a new address in another part of town where the women were meeting that night, but by then I'd had it. I was in no shape to make yet another 30-minute drive to another house I didn't know in order to arrive 45 minutes late to a Bible study of women I was beginning to doubt even wanted me in the first place.

I burst into tears. Like a crazy woman. Yes, I did. I couldn't help it, and I have no idea what I said to that man, but somehow I made it back to my car. All the emotional weight of our move came crashing down on me, and at that moment I felt like I didn't have a friend in the world. I had to wait a few minutes to calm down enough to drive, and by the time I got home, I was fuming.

"I know women are busy, and anyone can make a mistake, but two weeks in a row?!" I said to my husband. "I'm definitely not feeling the love from this group!"

That very minute, my phone beeped with a text message from my son.

"I love you, Mom," it said.

And I know it was God breaking through to me. Eighteen-year-old boys don't often text their moms out of the blue to say, "I love you," but at that moment, God had a message for me. And I believe I recognized His voice during my desperate moment partly because I'd spent time reading His Word to listen for His voice that morning and many mornings for the past 35 years. The more I practice listening to God in the morning, the more I am able to hear Him later in the day.

The more I practice listening to God in the morning, the more I am able to hear Him later in the day.

SMALL STEPS TOWARDS MORE

I'm sure you need more of God breaking through in your everyday life too, so I wrote this book to share with you some of my personal journey of discovering how to give the Lord more of my time and attention. For me, showing up to spend even a few minutes with God daily has been the most life-transforming practice of my Christian life. Even though sometimes, I blast out of bed and start my day without stopping to listen to my Lord first, I get back to it as soon as I can. Over time I've seen the rewards of showing up: a closer walk with Jesus, a stronger faith, and a wee bit more of His joy, peace, and love inside me. When we give God more time and attention, He gives us more of Himself.

I love Lysa TerKeurst's concept of "imperfect progress." In her book *Unglued*, Lysa invites readers to let go of beating themselves up over failure and embrace the idea of making imperfect progress towards better relationships with others.[1] Imperfect progress is a helpful thought for our relationship with God, as well, don't you think? We may not be rocking the church lady thing, we may have spent 15 minutes this morning zoned out in front of our Bibles, or we may have skipped that time altogether, but we can still make imperfect progress in our relationship with God. He is pleased with the smallest steps we make towards Him.

In this book, we explored the question of why spending time with God is important, and we looked at ways to find focus and open our doors to more of Him. We considered practices for getting more goodness from His Word and praying past distraction and discouragement. Lastly, we looked at how to take Jesus into our day and how to keep showing up to daily quiet time during difficult seasons.

Let's remember again God's promise to His people in Jeremiah 29:13. "You will seek me and find me when you seek me with all your heart." Notice the verse doesn't say, "You will find me when you have a devotional time without fail every day." It doesn't say, "You will find me when you start studying my word and finally learn to pray according to my will." No, God's only requirement is that we seek Him with all our hearts. The Lord sees our hearts as we take those faltering steps and make imperfect progress towards more of Him.

THE REWARDS WE'LL REAP

The biggest reward from showing up to spend time with God is a closer, clearer sense of His person and presence. We come to know our Lord better and learn to recognize His voice as we read His words and respond in prayer. The God who created the heavens and walks on the wings of the wind reveals Himself to us. When we keep His

Word close and walk in His commands, He comes and makes His home with us. As we stop to rest a few minutes in His presence each day, we realize all over again we are not alone. We have a Helper, the Holy Spirit, so we don't have to live like orphans left to scramble through life on their own. We have a Heavenly Father who is with us always.

The biggest reward from showing up to spend time with God is a clearer sense of His person and presence.

Showing up for more of God means more faith and less floundering. Psalm 9:10 reminds us: "Those who know your name trust in you, for you, LORD, have never forsaken those who seek you." In Scripture, God's "name" refers to His character and qualities. The more we know Him, the more we trust Him. As we read of His faithfulness and love on the pages of Scripture, our confidence in Him grows.

Hope grows along with an increasing sense of God's presence; He will never leave us. Faith and assurance of His love increase when we see tangible answers to our prayer or experience the conviction that He hears us yet waits for the right timing to work out His perfect design for us.

TRANSFORMED LIVES

More of God means a transformed life and the power to live out our faith. After all, the goal of our spiritual lives goes beyond an encouraging quiet time. We long to know Jesus better and look more like Him. A principle we all see played out in real life is that who you spend time with affects who you become. Don't you notice it too? When you hang out with people, they rub off on you. You start to share similar interests, talk like them, and even act like them. It's the same way with our Savior; the more time we spend with Him, the more we become like Him. I want to look more like Jesus, don't you? I long to live a life transformed by His joy, peace, and love.

The more time we spend with Jesus, the more we become like Him.

More of God means more joy and less angst, and we could all use more joy, right? Joy comes from the presence of God, and it not only makes us happier people, it also makes us more winsome to those around us. On my own, I'm not always such an attractive person, and that point was driven home to me recently.

"Mom, you seem stressed-out a lot of the time lately," my daughter said. "Is everything okay?" She said it in a matter of fact tone while I hurriedly prepared lunch one day, but it stopped me in my tracks. *Stressed out? What about life, peace, and joy in the Holy Spirit? What was I projecting to my loved ones? Was I really stressed out a lot of the time?*

My daughter's question woke me up to remember how I need to reconnect with Jesus constantly for more of His joy in me. Of course, having my quiet time doesn't guarantee I'll feel more joy that day, but it surely does help me set my mind on the Spirit in order to experience more life and peace.

More of God means more peace and less fretting. Jesus reassures us: "Peace I leave with you; my peace I give you. I do not give to you as the world gives. Do not let your hearts be troubled and do not be afraid" (John 14:27). We all long to walk in that perfect peace Jesus promises, and we know how useless it is to trouble our hearts by rehearsing fretful thoughts and worries in our minds. Yet we do it all the time, don't we? Allowing worry to work itself down deep into our minds, we latch on to fearful thoughts and repeat them to ourselves again and again. However, we can learn to calm and quiet our hearts in Jesus' presence each morning, and we can take baby steps back to that peaceful presence later during the day.

Lately the brief default prayers I write during my quiet time save me on many a fret-filled day. I notice that while I pray for something in the morning, I feel peaceful and confident that my Father will work it out. Yet later in the day while I'm busy with my tasks, Jesus seems further away, and I return to my fears and desperate attempts to control or manage difficult situations.

A one-sentence prayer I wrote helps me return to my peaceful place, and I try to repeat it when I go back to worry and control after I've already prayed for something.

"Lord, today I will let go of control and trust that You are caring for ..."

I complete my prayer with the name of the person or situation I'm thinking about. Some measure of peace returns to me when I return to Jesus in my thoughts.

Maybe the biggest reward I receive from giving God a bit more of my attention and time is more of His love in me. God is love, and that quiet moment in the morning to be still and know He is God reassures me that I am loved. I often repeat the words of Romans 5:5 to myself: "And hope does not put us to shame, because God's love has been poured out into our hearts through the Holy Spirit, who has been given to us."

When we make time to sit in the presence of the Holy Spirit, who pours love into our hearts, it leads to a greater sense of God's love later in the day. We have an easier time recognizing the signs of His love when He shows up to our desperate places, like He did for me during my failed attempt to find connection at a women's Bible study. When I got that text message, I knew deep in my heart God was reaching out to me with a message of love and care.

More of God's love in me leads to renewed transformation and change in how I respond and react to others. I am indebted to Rachel Macy Stafford and her book *Only Love Today*, which touched me in deep ways as I read her brief chapters many mornings after finishing my quiet time.[2] *Only Love Today* reminded me all over again that the best way I can reflect God to others is to love them well. Many mornings I pray, "Only love today, God." It helps me remember to intentionally receive God's love when I'm tempted to bash myself for failures, and it reminds me to show the Lord's love to my people when they drive me crazy.

That prayer "Only love today" opened a door for God and saved my attitude when my dear husband made a mistake that almost caused us to miss the flight to our once-in-a-lifetime trip to Rome. Our simple lifestyle and modest budget don't usually permit us to travel, but God blessed us with cheap flights and a free hotel to make this trip possible. We were celebrating our daughter's high school graduation. My husband always arranges our flights and lets us know what time we need to leave the house. To save money, we'd planned to take the metro to the airport instead of a taxi that morning. As we walked out of the house at 8 a.m., I glanced at my ticket and realized we did not have time to make a one-hour journey and check in for a flight that left at 9:30 am.

My husband had somehow miscalculated the time, so we scrambled to catch a taxi and stop at an ATM machine to take out cash to pay for it. As our driver fought morning traffic, we hunkered down to stay calm. Most likely, not even the bravest taxi driver could get us there on time. I knew we couldn't rebook our economy tickets, and I wondered if the trip we'd all looked forward to would end before it began.

"I don't know what I was thinking," my husband said, and I wondered myself. I had no idea how he'd thought we could leave our house 1.5 hours before takeoff time to travel across a city of 4 million people to the airport, but somehow I managed to hold my tongue. After all, it was an honest mistake I could have made myself. My normal response would be to berate my husband and sit fuming with thoughts of "If only…" Instead, by some miracle, I focused on breathing in and out, praying "Only love today, Lord" all the way to the airport. I hardly opened my mouth. I just prayed.

Miraculously, our taxi driver made the 45-minute drive in 20 minutes, and we boarded our flight and had the time of our lives for three days in Rome. I felt thankful that a small bit of prayer I'd repeated daily at the end of my quiet time made itself into one of my desperate moments and helped me open myself up to the guidance of the Holy Spirit. I also felt grateful because the glitch that started off our trip resolved itself quickly without me magnifying the situation by fretting, fuming, and creating more tension for all of us. I could have easily let a desperate moment distract me from opening the door to more of God, but He gave me the grace I needed when I opened one small door in the form of that one-sentence prayer.

YOUR JOURNEY FORWARD

I imagine that like me, you need more of God in your desperate places too. In fact, often those very moments when we need God most are also when we're most distracted. Frustration in the heat of a bad moment, worry, anxiety, and busy schedules can distract us from living out a relationship with God that brings more love, joy, peace, and Holy Spirit control into our lives. But we don't have to live in a state of unrelenting overwhelm and stress. Instead, we can press the pause button on our busy lives and learn to calm and quiet our souls, one baby step at a time. When we call on Him, Jesus turns our desperate places into doorways to His presence.

When we call on Jesus, He turns our desperate places into doorways to His presence.

Your small steps may look different than mine because you are on a different journey to more of God. Your way of relating to our Lord is unique to you, and you battle different distractions. I hope you've been encouraged as I've shared my attempts to overcome spiritual attention deficit and focus on growing a stronger connection with God to experience more of Him in my daily life.

I truly believe the most powerful step we can take is to set aside 20 minutes for our Lord each morning. When we make time to invite Him to be present and speak to us as we read His Word, we're opening a door for God. That door we open in the morning carries a ripple effect into our day; it prepares us to sense more of His presence later. Throughout the day we continue opening doors when we hum a song under our breath, lift up a brief prayer, pause to notice the miracle of a flower, or return to a verse we jotted down in on a card. We thank Him for a beautiful sunset or read a Psalm before bed. God is pleased with our small efforts to turn towards Him.

Even the littlest windows we open usher God's powerful presence into our lives. When we invite Him in,

He comes. He comes bringing more of Himself: more light, love, and power into our lives.

Even the littlest windows we open usher God's powerful presence into our lives.

Friend, I started this book by telling you I don't really rock the church lady thing, and maybe you don't either. But we can breathe easier because God isn't looking for perfect church ladies. He's looking for women who will seek Him despite themselves, women who will return to Him a thousand times when they find they've drifted away. He's looking for the woman who will decide that today is the day to open His Word even if she hasn't read it in two weeks. He's looking for a woman who will take a prayer walk on her lunch hour although she skipped her quiet time in the morning, and He's looking for the woman who will wring out a prayer today though she hasn't prayed in years. He's looking for that woman who will open up a Psalm to read aloud because that's about all she can handle right now.

God is looking for women who want more of Him. He's looking for a woman like you.

God is looking for women who want more of Him, women who will treasure His Word and attempt to live by it. He's looking for a woman like you. Friend, today is your day. As you take even the smallest steps towards God today, He'll be pleased because He loves you more than you know. And He'll reward you with more of Himself.

Acknowledgements

I want to thank my family for supporting me and believing in me when I said I wanted to write a book. Instead of looking at me like I was Martian from outer space or a woman who'd lost her mind, my dear husband José acted like he thought it was the greatest idea ever. José, Andrés, and Camilla listened to me talk, ramble, and dream about this book for almost two years.

Thanks to my dear friend Alev Tison, who suggested I start writing ten years ago and who rallied friends to give me a fabulous birthday gift in 2014: money to register for Proverbs 31 Ministries' She Speaks conference! I'll never forget it.

I am grateful for my online community of writing besties: Abby, Kristi, Kristine, Lisa, Lyli, and Tiffany. You girls kept me sane, prayed for me, and supported me through thick and thin when I thought about giving up writing and when I was stressed beyond words by the political climate my last two years in Turkey.

I am more grateful than I can say for Jan Herbert, who generously gifted me with her editing and proofreading expertise. She was a dramatic answer to prayer one Sunday when I prayed desperately in the morning, "Lord,

I need an editor!" and found myself sitting next to a professional editor at a restaurant later in the day.

Thanks also to my faith communities at Yaşayan Söz Kilisesi in Izmir and Hope Chapel in Austin. Many of you prayed for me and encouraged me. Zeynep, Jill, Nilva, Lyn, Anne, PJ, and Janet, everyone needs friends like you in their life. Thank you.

I'd also like to thank Proverbs 31 Ministries COMPEL Training community for providing training, encouragement, and fellowship for writers like me.

Last, but not least, I want to thank the believing women of Turkey. You have been my friends, my disciples, and my teachers in the pursuit of discovering more of God.

NOTES

Chapter 3: How 20 Minutes a Day Can Change Your Life

1. Robert Elmer and Brother Lawrence of the Resurrection, *Practicing God's Presence: Brother Lawrence for Today's Reader* (Colorado Springs, CO: Navpress, 2005).
2. Matt Redman, "Blessed Be Your Name," track 1 on *Blessed Be Your Name: The Songs of Matt Redman, Vol. 1*, Sparrow Records/Six Step Records, 2005.
3. Jan Johnson, *Enjoying the Presence of God: Discovering Intimacy with God in the Daily Rhythms of Life* (Colorado Springs, CO: Navpress, 1996), 126.

Chapter 5: Finding Focus

1. Beth Moore, *Stepping Up: A Journey Through the Psalms of Ascent* (Lifeway Press, 2007).
2. Pat Brett and Tony Brown, "Good Good Father," track 7 on *Housefires II*, Housefires, 2014.
3. Jason Ingram, Leslie Jordan, and David Leonard, "Great Are You Lord" track 8 on *All Sons and Daughters*, Columbia Records, 2014.

Chapter 6: Getting Goodness from God's Word

1. Kathryn Shirey, *Pray Deep* (Frisco, TX: San Marco Publications, 2015), 40.
2. Holly, July 20, 2017, Comment on author's Facebook ministry page, https://www.facebook.com/faithspillingover/.

Chapter 8: Making It Enjoyable

1. Katie, Carmen, and Elizabeth, Jun 22, 2017, Comments on author's personal Facebook page.
2. Jana Kennedy-Spicer, September 29, 2018, Bible Journaling Workshop attended by author. For more information, see Sweet to the Soul Facebook page, https://www.facebook.com/Sweet.To.The.Soul.Ministries/.

Chapter 9: Help for Distracted, Side-Tracked Prayer Warriors

1. Max Lucado, *Before Amen: The Power of a Simple Prayer* (Nashville, TN: Thomas Nelson, 2014), 1.
2. Trevor Miller, "Pray as You Can, Not as You Can't," *Northumbria Community*, https://www.northumbriacommunity.org/articles/pray-can-cant/.
3. Sybil MacBeth, *Praying in Color: Drawing a New Path to God* (Brewster, MA: Paraclete Press, 2007), 27.

Chapter 10: After Your Quiet Time: Taking Jesus with You into Your Day

1. Kathryn Shirey, *Pray Deep* (Frisco, TX: San Marco Publications, 2015), 51-52.
2. Betsy de Cruz, "One Simple Way to Pray on the Go," September 20, 2016, http://faithspillingover.com/2016/09/20/simple-way-to-pray-on-the-go/.

Chapter 11: How to Keep Going with God When Life Gets Hard

1. Lisa Appelo, "Life Shattered," June 5, 2014, https://lisaappelo.com/life-shattered/.
2. Lisa Appelo, "The Daily Exchange: My Thoughts for God's Thoughts," October 8, 2015, http://lisaappelo.com/the-daily-exchange-my-thoughts-for-gods-thoughts/.

Chapter 12: The Reward of Showing Up: More of God

1. Lysa TerKeurst, *Unglued: Making Wise Choices in the Midst of Raw Emotions* (Grand Rapids, MI: Zondervan, 2012), 14-15.
2. Rachel Macy Stafford, *Only Love Today: Reminders to Breathe More, Stress Less, and Choose Love* (Grand Rapids, MI: Zondervan, 2017), 13-14.

MEET BETSY

Betsy de Cruz has battled distraction in her relationship with God for over 20 years while serving in women's ministry, church planting, and child raising. Nothing thrills her heart more than inspiring women to pursue a deeper relationship with God and build their faith through His Word. She writes and speaks to encourage women to get more of God's Word in, so they can live their faith out.

You can find Betsy on her blog, faithspillingover.com, where she shares Bible study and prayer tips for distracted women, as well as encouragement for everyday faith and family. Betsy has also written numerous articles and devotionals online.

Betsy is married to José Cruz and has two children, Andrés and Camilla. She has spent most of her adult life in Central America and the Middle East, and her family recently moved back to Texas after 16 years in Turkey. When Betsy is not writing, she is drinking chai with Middle Eastern women in Austin.

CONNECT WITH BETSY

WEBSITE: Connect with Betsy at faithspillingover.com, where you'll find weekly devotional content and free resources to help you engage with God's Word and live it out.

SOCIAL MEDIA: You can follow Betsy for daily encouragement (and pictures of her life and family).

FACEBOOK:
https://www.facebook.com/faithspillingover
INSTAGRAM: @BetsydeCruz
TWITTER: @BetsydeCruz
PINTEREST: https://www.pinterest.com/betsydecruz/